THE
SWAN IN MY BATHTUB

THE SWAN IN MY BATHTUB

and Other Adventures in The Aark

Mary Jane Stretch
and Phyllis Hobe

A DUTTON BOOK

DUTTON
Published by the Penguin Group
Penguin Books USA Inc., 375 Hudson Street,
New York, New York 10014, U.S.A.
Penguin Books Ltd, 27 Wrights Lane,
London W8 5TZ, England
Penguin Books Australia Ltd, Ringwood,
Victoria, Australia
Penguin Books Canada Ltd, 2801 John Street,
Markham, Ontario, Canada L3R 1B4
Penguin Books (N.Z.) Ltd, 182-190 Wairau Road,
Auckland 10, New Zealand

Penguin Books Ltd, Registered Offices:
Harmondsworth, Middlesex, England

First published by Dutton, an imprint of New American Library, a division of
Penguin Books USA Inc.
Distributed in Canada by McClelland & Stewart Inc.

First Printing, June, 1991
10 9 8 7 6 5 4 3 2 1

 REGISTERED TRADEMARK—MARCA REGISTRADA

LIBRARY OF CONGRESS CATALOGING IN PUBLICATION DATA:

Stretch, Mary Jane.
    The swan in my bathtub and other tales from the Aark / Mary Jane Stretch
and Phyllis Hobe.
        p. cm.
    ISBN 0-525-24999-0
    1. Wildlife rehabilitation—Pennsylvania. 2. Aark (Foundation) 3. Stretch,
Mary Jane. 4 Animals—Anecdotes. 5. Wildlife rehabilitators—Pennsylvania—Biography. I. Hobe, Phyllis. II. Title.
SF996.45.S77   1991
639.9—dc20   90–24014
                                                                                 CIP

Printed in the United States of America
Set in Palatino
Designed by Eve L. Kirch

This book is dedicated to my mother, for teaching me to care, and to my father, for teaching me to value freedom for wild animals. These two perspectives form the basis of what I do and what I've done all my life.

Contents

Introduction

I met Mary Jane Stretch by way of a bird that fell out of a tall cedar tree right in front of my dog as we were walking near our house. The bird was very young and hopped around frantically, trying to get away from my dog's inquiring nose.

After I brought my dog into the house, I went out to look at the bird. It was still flopping on the ground. I looked up into the cedar tree and saw a nest tucked into a fork of branches. I had lived in the country only a few months, and I knew nothing about birds. But the bird seemed to be in trouble, and I wanted to help. I brought a ladder, climbed up, and put the tiny bird in the nest.

Ten minutes later, when I went back to take a look, the bird was on the ground again. I didn't know how to get help for a bird, so I called my veterinarian for advice. He told me to call The Aark.

"What's that?" I said.

"You'll find out," he told me.

When I dialed the number, a woman with a pleasant voice and an efficient manner told me exactly what to do: "If the bird is feathered and able to hop, it's ready

1

to fly. In that case, don't intervene. If it doesn't have feathers, it's too young to fly." She said the mother bird probably was nearby and would feed the baby. But, just in case something had happened to the mother bird, the woman told me how to feed the baby. She gave me a recipe that included canned dog food, wheat germ, and several other ingredients.

When I went outside again, I felt better prepared. But the bird was gone. Apparently it had flown.

A year later I had occasion to call The Aark again. A robin began attacking the windows in my garage. He kept beating himself against the glass and wouldn't come inside when I opened the windows. I was afraid the bird would injure himself. None of my neighbors had ever heard of such a thing, so they couldn't help. Then I remembered The Aark.

The same woman answered the phone. When I told her what was going on, she laughed and said, "Well, robins are very sexy birds, and this is the mating season. Next week I'll be getting calls about cardinals." She explained that the robin saw his reflection in the window glass and thought it was another male trying to invade his territory. The only thing I could do, she said, was to tape a blanket or some newspapers over the glass to obliterate a reflection. "You might have to live that way for quite some time," she cautioned.

She was right. I taped newspapers over both garage windows and the attacks ended. When I took them down a week later, the bird came back with a vengeance. He covered the entire side of my garage with excrement, which took forever to remove. Naturally the newspapers went back up—and remained there for a month.

When I called to report that all was quiet again, I asked the woman her name. She was Mary Jane Stretch, the founder of The Aark, a wildlife rehabilitation center located in Newtown, Pennsylvania. A few weeks later I went to The Aark because my cat brought home a badly mauled rabbit. Mary Jane said I should bring it to her.

She would do what she could or, if necessary, put it down humanely.

I followed her instructions. I put the rabbit in a cardboard box and tucked a soft towel around it. Then I drove to The Aark, which is about thirty-five miles from my home.

Driving down the narrow road leading to The Aark is not like entering another world, but rather like entering our own world as most of us wish it could be. I drove slowly because all sorts of birds and animals crossed my path—a marvelous variety of geese and ducks, the little ones (and some of the big ones) waddling up wooden boards to plunge into children's wading pools; some ring-necked pheasants and a wild turkey taking seeds from a huge, shallow pan near the barn; and, under some trees, a fawn nibbling at the grass. Off to one side I could see wood-framed structures, one-story high and sided with wire screening. I heard squawks that sounded like the hawks in my neighborhood.

Mary Jane was in the intensive care room on the first floor of the handsome old house that is both her residence and a hospital for orphaned and injured wildlife. She had just put a baby 'possum into an incubator that already had several other young 'possums nestled close together and wrapped in soft towels. The animals looked helpless, yet secure, as if they sensed that someone was looking after them. A staff member sat at a desk along one wall. She was recording the new patient's vital statistics.

As soon as Mary Jane saw the box I was carrying, she took it from me. There was something exceptional in the way she handled the hurt rabbit. I've always believed that some people have healing in their hands, and she definitely did. The rabbit yielded to her touch and stopped trembling. It crouched, absolutely still, while she examined its body for wounds. She found one—a nasty puncture—in the rabbit's side.

"He won't make it," she told me. "Rabbits are especially vulnerable to trauma, and this is a bad wound.

He'll live for thirty-six hours at most, and then he'll die. Or—I can put him down now. It's up to you."

I didn't know what to say. There were two questions I wanted to ask, but I had difficulty putting them into words. Mary Jane seemed to know what they were and answered them.

"If he lives thirty-six hours, they won't be good ones," she said. "If I put him down, I'll do it gently."

"Yes," I told her. "Please—do it."

She took the rabbit into another room.

"Would you like your towel back?" the young woman at the desk asked me.

I really was very upset. My thoughts, my whole being, were with the rabbit, wishing I had been able to do something to change the course of events. "No," I said. Suddenly, the towel—giving the towel—was an important gesture of helpfulness. "Can you use it?"

"We sure can," the young woman said. "Thanks."

I wanted to wait. And while I did, I looked at the incubators. The 'possums were in one, tiny rabbits in another, and fuzzy-headed young birds in the third. "What are these?" I asked, pointing to the birds.

"Kestrels," the young woman said. When she saw that I didn't know what a kestrel was, she explained that they were sparrow hawks. "A man brought in the whole nest—something happened to the parents."

Looking at so many small, helpless, living creatures that had a chance to make it somewhat balanced the little rabbit that didn't. I realized that while I loved the country and was concerned about our environment, I knew little about the natural world. I saw animals and birds dead along the road as I drove, but to me they were facts of life. There were animals and there were cars, and such things happened. I didn't like it, but I didn't know what I could do about it. I saw fields of tall grass and thorny weeds cut down to make way for smooth lawns kept uniformly green with showers of chemicals, but that seemed to be what people wanted. I hadn't considered how our civilized tastes threaten the very existence of wild animals and birds—or how their existence is a part of mine. Not many of us do. It made me feel better about myself as a human being to discover that some people not only care what happens to wild creatures but actually know how to help them when the rest of us push them around.

Before I went home that day, I asked Mary Jane how I could do something practical with my good feelings. Her suggestions were easy to follow. My cat wears a collar with a bell on it now. It doesn't seem to bother him, and it gives some wild animals a better chance at life. I set out birdfeeders and birdbaths, and as I watch the activity around them, I learn how one generation teaches the skills of survival to another. Living becomes more than a matter of my own existence; I am part of something much greater. When persistent heavy rains turn part of my property into a swamp and make mowing impossible, I don't worry about the height of the grass. I know the wetland will attract and feed waterthrushes, birds I normally don't see. I'm finding safe substitutes for the chemicals I used in my garden. I am discovering how I fit into the whole of life on earth. I am realizing that life does not begin and end with me; it began long before I existed and, I hope, will go on long after I am gone.

The Swan in My Bathtub is the result of my interest in and inquiry into The Aark and the woman who made it possible. It is intended to share with as many others as possible some of the awareness that I experienced personally:

That life is precious in all its forms,

That human survival is related to the survival of all other living creatures,

That each of us can do something to slow or stop the destruction of our universe.

—Phyllis Hobe

I / "Whose Birds Are These?"

The fledgling tree is a big old pine that grows right along-side the house where I live and work. I can't imagine how any tree could grow to suit my needs so perfectly, but somehow this one did—and long before I came here. When I moved into the house during the seventies, the shrubs and other trees had grown over the windows on both floors and all the way up to the roof. Little by little my daughters and I cut them back to let some light into the house, and one day we hacked our way through to the tree.

I had known that an evergreen was back there. I could see its needles poking through the jungle in front of it. But *such* a tree! I stepped back in admiration. "It's a fledgling tree!" I said to the girls. "This is where we'll put the baby birds when they're ready to fly."

My daughters were not impressed. It was hot, and they had better things to do. Besides, there was always that little irritation whenever I turned my attention to my wild offspring. Like all children, mine did not want to share their mother. They did not, and still do not, know quite how to deal with the thousands of animals and birds who have rightfully claimed me as a mother of sorts. I do not agree with my daughters when they say that my work deprives them of me; they have always come first, and I think they know that. But when you're a wildlife rehabilitator, you don't work regular hours and then quit. The need is always there, and you do what has to be done.

"Okay, we'll knock off for now," I said, and immediately Debbie and Leah disappeared around the side of the house. They were fourteen and ten at the time, quite independent. But Sammy was only six, and was too young to tag along with her sisters or go off on her own. Since she did not like being restricted, I tried to interest her in the tree.

"See, Sammy," I said, running my hand along the thick branch that grew downward at a steep angle from the main trunk and then leveled off for a few feet before it turned upward again. "This is just right for the baby birds. It's only about three feet off the ground, so they can fly up here easily. Then they can sit on the branch until they're ready to go higher or back down." The level part of the branch was bare of needles and looked like a mighty brown bicep, a good four inches across. A fledgling would feel secure there. And at the very end of the branch, where it turned upward again, was thick foliage. A bird could hide there.

I felt as if the tree had been waiting for me—and for The Aark, the name I had chosen for the wildlife rehabilitation center I was going to open. Originally I intended to spell *Ark* correctly, but someone else was using it, although not in connection with wildlife. "Why don't you spell it A-a-r-k," Debbie suggested. "You never spell anything right, anyway," she giggled. It was a good idea. Adding the second *a* made it okay for us to be The Aark.

Over the years, word of The Aark has spread beyond our Pennsylvania home into neighboring states. People bring us orphaned and injured birds and wild animals from all over. We try to heal them and return them to their natural habitat. We treat over thirty-five hundred creatures a year, and many of them are young birds who haven't yet flown.

People often ask me how I teach a bird to fly, and my answer always is "I don't. I just give them the opportunity." You do not teach a bird to fly; they fly when they're ready. Some birds, such as swallows, hawks, and Eastern kingbirds, leave the nest in full flight. But most birds need to flutter-fly first. And this is where the fledgling tree comes in.

When I see that our young birds are ready to fly, I begin taking them out of the nursery during the day. I bring them out to the fledgling tree at seven o'clock each morning and put them in two large pens under the tree. The pens are made of wood, with a solid top and back, and wire screening on three sides, which allows plenty of room for several birds to hop around freely. The birds are accustomed to being fed by me, so when I open the pen doors, they come and go as they feed. I don't leave the pens open—I close the doors when I'm finished feeding the birds—but since I feed them every hour until nightfall, they have many opportunities to fly.

The minute a bird flutters up on my shoulder instead of staying on the ground, it begins to stay out for the rest of the day. I take it off my shoulder and put it on the wide branch of the fledgling tree. Some birds will flutter straight up to the tree on their own. If a bird stays on the ground, then it's not ready to fly, so I put it back in the pen and close the door until the next feeding time. It takes a couple of days for most birds to get the hang of flying, but it's important for them to go through the process. It recreates the experience of leaving the nest.

When most birds leave the nest, they flutter-fly from branch to branch, down, then higher up, sometimes hopping, sometimes fluttering, eventually flying. All the while the mother and father birds follow them and feed them, listening for their cries, which they can distinguish from those of any other birds. The babies also know their parents' voices.

Our little orphaned birds know my voice. They associate it with food and protection. When I come out to feed them each hour, I always speak to them. If they aren't already waiting for me on the big branch, they fly down from higher branches. Then I open the pens to see who else wants to leave.

At first the fledglings don't move far from the big branch, but as soon as they have any kind of flight at all, they become real hotshots. Their attitude is "I don't need you—I don't need to be fed." They zoom from the branch to the shrubs to the fence, back and forth, and then they fly higher up into the tree. If they fly too high the first time, they often don't know how to come back down. It may take them all day. But by nighttime, when I bring them all in, they're down. Or, the next morning, when I open the door, there they are, sitting on the step.

In their natural habitat, as fledglings begin to feed themselves, they develop their flying skills. Then the parents stop following them. Instead, the fledglings follow the voices of the parents, and, for a while, even though they can feed themselves, they demand to be fed. If you've ever watched what goes on at a birdfeeder, you'll often see a mother bird feeding a baby that's bigger than she is, and she does it with an attitude of "Oh, all *right!*" Gradually she makes it harder for the baby to get food from her, until finally the baby is on its own. Or, if the baby continues to pester for food, the mother will drive it off or fly away.

When our babies learn to fly well, they also begin to feed themselves. Quite often they'll bring me the first bug they catch, because they don't know what to do with it. They're very excited about it, but it's all mushy in their mouths. I give it back to them, and then they know what to do with it. After a few more tries, they begin to connect catching the bug with swallowing it. For a while they may still want me to feed them, too, and I do. But finally they leave. Wild things prefer their own habitat. At least most of them do—but there's always the exception.

Spring is the start of The Aark's busy season. Birds and animals begin giving birth, and unfortunate intrusions can threaten the lives of their young. They get hit by cars, and mauled by dogs and cats or by other wild animals. Sometimes they lose a parent before they're old enough to feed themselves. Sometimes a parent abandons them because there isn't enough food to go around—or there's something wrong with the baby. Survival is so chancy in the wild world that there isn't time to fix whatever doesn't work right. But sometimes wildlife rehabbers can help—if we get to the unfortunate ones in time.

A few years ago a woman brought in a very young bluejay. She had found it along the road under a tree, and immediately she knew there was something wrong with it.

"The elbows look funny," she said, pointing to the bird's legs. Instead of being bent back under the bird's body, they stuck out to each side and the bird couldn't stand. "Shouldn't they bend the other way?" the woman asked.

"Actually they're not elbows," I said, "although they do look like them. That part of the leg—from the toes to that elbowlike joint—that's the foot. The elbow-like joint is the heel, and the bird should be squatting down on it."

"Will it be all right?" the woman wanted to know. "Can you help it?"

"Probably," I told her. I asked Rosalie, one of our volunteers, to make out a card for the bird while I took it into the nursery. It was no more than three or four days old, a baby that belonged in a nest. The bird looked kind of naked; its feathers were just coming out of their feather cases. The casings looked like tiny blue straws here and there on the bird's body, and inside each casing was a blue feather. The odd-looking legs were still soft, but they would harden. We had to correct the deformity before the legs hardened in that outlandish position, though, or the bird would never be able to stand. Or fly. Time, vitamins, and proper diet would help, but the most important thing we had to do was recreate a good nest environment.

If you've ever looked into an occupied bird's nest, you probably thought it was too small because the birds were so crowded. They seemed too big for the nest. But when birds are born, they're so floppy that they might as well be put together with rubber bands. They need to be crowded in order to keep their legs under them until they harden in the proper position. Actually, the babies sit on their heels until they grow strong enough to lift themselves up and stand on their toes. If their legs aren't crowded and kept under them while they're soft, they'll stick out to the sides and the bird will be sprawl-legged, just like our little orphan.

I had no way of knowing what went on in its nest. Maybe the mother's other eggs didn't hatch, and the only surviving baby wasn't crowded enough to develop properly. Maybe the mother's food supply was faulty or she had trouble getting enough to feed all her young. In any event, she probably pitched this little one out. In the wild world, that's often the only solution.

I wasn't able to put the bird in an isolette because in those days we had only one and it was already occupied by baby mammals. The next best place for it was a snake box, which is made of wood except for the top and front panels. The top is screened to allow for ventilation and the front is made of glass so the bird or animal can be observed without disturbing it. I put a heating pad in the box and shaped it into a U along the back panel.

Next I folded a diaper and tucked it into a small bread-basket. That was going to be the bluejay's nest. When I placed the bird in it, I made sure that its legs were properly positioned under its body, and then I pulled the diaper up and around its legs, crowding them as if the bird were in its natural nest, surrounded by closely-packed siblings. Overcrowding also keeps baby birds warm, and the mother spends a lot of time sitting on them for that same reason, but for now the heating pad would have to do. I put the breadbasket and its only inhabitant in a corner of the box.

Rosalie came in while I was feeding our new patient some of our own recipe for baby birds. "What do you suppose we've got there, a male or a female?" she asked.

I dipped a child's water-color paintbrush into the food and guided it into the gaping mouth. Then I brushed the food against the back of the bird's throat. "We'll have to wait and see," I said. It's impossible to distinguish male from female bluejays. "Unfortunately, it's going to need overhandling."

Ordinarily I don't like to handle our patients any more than absolutely necessary. It makes them too trusting of human beings, and it's that much harder for them to make it when they go back into their world. Man is more often an enemy than a friend to wild things, and most wild things know it. Their caution helps them to survive, and I don't like to interfere with it. But we had to check the crowding of the diaper around the bluejay's legs at least every hour, and that meant we would have to handle it more than usual. I hoped that our gentleness would not persuade the bird to give up its wariness about being touched.

The bluejay began to show improvement within four or five days. As its legs hardened under its body, the bird moved its weight forward and squatted on its toes. Its feathers grew out of their cases, covering its body with beautiful shades of blue and gray. Soon it would be ready to fly; the development of a bird from hatch-time to flight is incredibly swift.

I took the baby out to the fledgling tree along with

several other young birds, and two days later it was flying and beginning to feed itself. Then it left, and as hard
as it was to let the bird go, that was exactly what I
wanted it to do. Most of our patients go back into the
ecosystem, and we don't know what happens to them
there. If you're a sensitive human being, that uncertainty
can hurt. Probably half of them will die of natural
causes—but that's what they're supposed to do. At least
they're not dying because they were hit by a car or
because their food supply was wiped out by pesticides
or a developer leveling the land. Rehabbers can't *make*
wild things live. We can only give them another chance
to complete a natural life cycle.

By early fall there were fewer fledglings to bring out
to the tree, and soon there were none. The breeding season was over. Finally we brought the pens in and put
them away.

One morning late in November I heard a tapping on
the dining-room window. I looked out and saw a lovely
blue-jay. The bird was quite insistent, so I went to the
back door, taking a dish of seeds with me. When I
opened the door, there was the bird on the step. Without
hesitation it came inside. It flew up to my shoulder and
then perched on my hand. I poured some seeds in the
palm of my other hand and the bird ate some. Most wild
birds won't do that. Could it be—? Was it—? I don't
pretend to be able to identify one bluejay from another
by sight, but sometimes I can distinguish one bird from
another by its behavior patterns. And I was certain this
was the little sprawl-legged baby bluejay we had healed
the past summer. That bird had eaten from my hand,
too; in packing the diaper around its legs, I overhandled
it so much, that it lost all fear of me.

When the bluejay had enough to eat, it wanted to
leave, and I opened the door for it. But the next morning
it was back, this time tapping at the kitchen window over
the sink where I was rinsing some dishes. I opened the

window and in came the bird. It ate and left. It came every day after that, always at the same time and in all kinds of weather.

Then one day it didn't show up. I began looking out the windows on all sides of the house, hoping to catch sight of it. I went out to the fledgling tree but it was empty. I tried not to worry, but I couldn't help myself. Overhandling had its effect on me, too.

Two more days passed and the bluejay didn't come back. Maybe it finally decided to leave for the winter. But maybe—I didn't want to think about other possibilities.

On the fourth day one of my neighbors called me up. "Are you missing a bird?" he asked.

I said, "Is it a bluejay?"

"Yes, yes!" he said. "It's a bluejay. I figured it must be yours because it's doing things I never saw a bluejay do. It comes to my window and taps on it. When I open the window, the bird jumps in. It eats sunflower seeds right out of my hand!"

"Ohmigosh!" I said. I was so relieved.

"I named her Peggy," my neighbor said. "Is that all right?"

"It's lovely," I told him. "But I'm not sure it's a female."

From then on, I called her Peggy, too. So many wild creatures come and go at The Aark that I try not to name them. That way it's easier for me to let them go. Besides, where would I find enough names for the thousands of birds and animals we treat? But Peggy was special. And apparently she wasn't going to leave. At least not that winter.

She began coming back to see me every day, and she continued to visit my neighbor as well. Then another neighbor called to ask me if one of my birds was missing. It seems a bluejay tapped on her window and came inside to eat out of her hand.

"Her name is Peggy," I explained, "and I'm aware that

she's gone. It's okay for you to feed her. But, please, don't take her into the house. Let her leave as soon as she wants to." I was concerned that Peggy's new friends might encourage her to stay indoors on a cold or rainy day, and that wasn't a good idea. "When she's ready to go, she's ready, period," I said. "If you don't let her out, she might panic and crash into a window. That could kill her."

Peggy made the rounds that winter, treating all of us to the thrill of having a lovely bird fly down out of the sky, eat out of our hands, and fly off again. My two neighbors lived almost a half-mile away, but Peggy would visit one, then the other, and finally she'd come to The Aark. She was so punctual that I could look at my watch and say, "Well, Peggy's due in." She'd fly in, sit on my hand, and eat some seeds, but she wouldn't allow me to hold her. That was a good sign. Then, early the next spring, we stopped seeing her. This time I wasn't worried. I assumed she was starting a family.

One morning about a month later, when we were setting baby birds on the fledgling tree during the day, I found two little bluejay fledglings sitting on the big branch. I wondered how they got there, because I didn't remember bringing any bluejays out the day before. That upset me. I thought someone had put the birds out there without giving them a chance to go in and out of the pen and be fed. The security of being fed helps the bird to venture into flight. First things first!

The two newcomers took food from me as readily as the other fledglings. As soon as I fed them, I went into the office to look through the admission cards. I was angry. It was a hot day, and I was tired because I had been up most of the night with an injured 'possum. My temper was short. I couldn't find a card for any bluejays, and there were none in the nursery. "Now what?" I thought. "Someone not only left them out there, but didn't even card them in!"

I called in the volunteers and said, "We've got two fledgling bluejays out there, but no card for them. What's the story?"

All I got were puzzled looks and shrugging shoulders. "They should be in the pen before they go on the branch," I told them. I didn't like the sharpness in my voice and tried to tone it down. "I thought you knew that," I said. "It doesn't take much time for them to make the connection, but it's something they absolutely have to do. You can't take shortcuts."

The response was unanimous:

"I didn't put them out there."

"I didn't do it."

"I didn't even know we had any bluejays."

Embarrassment began to replace my anger. I was running out of people, and we still couldn't account for the fledgling bluejays. Frustrated, I went out to the tree again, and there they were, their mouths wide open, ready to eat again.

All of a sudden an adult bluejay came swooping down out of the tree and sat next to the babies. Apparently it was the fledglings' mother. She fed them a bug she had brought with her. Then she sat on my hand and squawked excitedly. She didn't want me to hold her, yet she allowed me to hold the fledglings. It was too much to believe! I was so excited that I thought, "I want this so badly that I'm just making the pieces fit. It can't really be Peggy!"

But I knew it was by the way the bird behaved. She squawked on and on, as if she had so much news to tell me, and then she flew away. She left the fledglings with me. Now, when I was a little girl and my mother needed a break from her kids, she'd take us to Granny's and leave us there for the day. I wondered if bluejay mothers did the same thing. Maybe I was the granny in Peggy's life. I fed the little guys every hour all that day and watched them fly from branch to branch. They were quite accomplished.

It was almost dark when Peggy returned. "Well," I said to her, "did you have a good time?" She sat on my shoulder and then she flew off, taking the fledglings with her. She never brought them back again. But she continued to visit my neighbors and me for a few more winters. Then, last year, we didn't see her. In the wild world, that's often the way good-byes are said.

2 / Becoming a Pro

How I came to The Aark, and how The Aark itself came to be, is a story of surprises. I didn't plan any of it.

I have always loved and worked with birds and animals. As a very young child, I spent most of my time playing in the woods around my parents' home in Bucks County, Pennsylvania, when it was much less developed than it is now. I never had any intention of making nature my vocation because I didn't think such a thing was possible. The few wildlife rehabilitators I heard of did it for nothing—not because they enjoyed going hungry, but because nobody had enough money to pay them. In the long list of modern man's priorities, wild things are pretty close to the bottom.

As long as I didn't have to earn a living, I was able to rehabilitate a growing army of small creatures. Wherever I lived—with my parents and, later, with my husband and children in southern New Jersey—the rooms of our house were cluttered with boxes and cages housing patients of all kinds and sizes. Each one was on a different feeding schedule, and I refused to ignore it or turn it over to someone who might not think it was important to be punctual.

For a while, at the beginning of my married life, I gave up my "practice." But it seemed to follow me. As the saying goes, "When you're ready for your teacher, it will appear." When the animals were ready for their healer, they and I met. Someone would bring me a bird with a broken wing or a baby raccoon that was too young to survive on its own. I simply did what I felt had to be done. I didn't always know the solution intellectually. Quite often it came from somewhere within—or possibly from without. I seem to have a gift, but what it is, and exactly where it comes from, I can't say. I do believe there are powers of healing in the universe and, if we keep ourselves spiritually open, we can serve as channels for them.

I wasn't always able to save a bird or an animal, but I could sometimes, and the word got around that somebody in the neighborhood knew what to do with an orphaned or injured creature. My patients multiplied, and so did the boxes and cages. If I wanted to go somewhere and it interfered with feeding schedules, I took my patients along with me in the back of my station wagon.

In 1962 my young husband died of cancer, and suddenly I was a single mother with a two-year-old daughter to raise. It was not at all the kind of future I had anticipated, and I wasn't prepared. I hadn't been brought up to think about a career, and in my family girls weren't considered particularly competent. I had been an art major in college, but had married at nineteen and didn't continue my education.

I had a small income from my late husband's estate. For a few years it was enough for Debbie and me to get by on—barely. But I had many other mouths to feed: squirrels, foxes, 'possums, skunks, groundhogs, mice, geese, owls, robins, bluejays, crows, wrens, owls. As fast as I returned them to the wild, new ones came in. There wasn't enough money to feed all of us, so I did housework to pay for the birdseed. And in time I married again and had two more daughters.

My daughters are quite different from each other, yet I can see something of myself in each one of them. Debbie, the oldest, has light red hair and green eyes. I chose the name Deborah because it's a strong name, and she was born at a time when I had to be strong. Debbie has always been a strong person. She's serious and both her feet are firmly on the ground, but she doesn't miss the clouds. She's the most contented human being I have ever known.

Leah, four years younger, was born at a happy time in my life. She seems to embody the joy I feel at being alive. Her name means "light," and she lives up to it. She's blond, blue-eyed, and filled with light. She sees the good in everything. When she was little I used to tell her that I found her under a May Apple. She'd ask me what that was, and I'd explain that a May Apple is one of the first plants to flower in the spring. A white waxy flower blooms under its leaves, and fairies are said to leave children there for human beings to find and love. Leah looks just like a child the fairies might have left under a May Apple for me to find. But I used to tell her that a little too often. Years later she confessed that when she was a child she thought she was adopted.

Sammy is four years younger than Leah. She's my dark child. She has dark hair and eyes, and she's stormy, moody, mystical, and extremely intelligent. Like me, she analyzes everything, and my simplest comment can lead the two of us into an hourlong discussion of universal truths. But she also has a wonderful sense of humor. I named her Samantha George after both her grandparents because I wanted someone in our family to carry their names into the future. Sammy does it beautifully.

Several years after Sammy was born, I was a divorced mother of three. I knew I needed a full-time job, but it was hard for me to give up being with my daughters. While they were very young, I was able to be home with them, and I loved it. I loved holding them, talking to them, feeding them. I never left them alone in a playpen; before they could walk, I carried them wherever I went around the house. But when they were ready to discover their world for themselves, I didn't try to hold them back.

All three girls were in school when I decided to look for a full-time job. By then my work with children of the wild was attracting attention, not all of it welcome. I got calls and letters from cults wanting to know what kind of supernatural powers I was using to heal my patients; and a few even called me a witch. My daughters endured a lot of teasing, and some children in the neighborhood were forbidden to play with them. Ecology wasn't considered chic in those days, so my concern for it was considered sort of nutty. The writers of some of the newspaper articles were more enlightened; they gave me an opportunity to spread some advice about birds and animals in trouble—when to leave them alone, when to intervene, how to handle them, and why it's important to return them to their natural environment whenever possible. Sometimes people with the best intentions do the worst kinds of things.

For a little while I was a part-time volunteer on a research project for the Trenton Museum. We didn't rehabilitate wild things there, but we observed them and recorded details of their behavior and development. That's when I discovered, quite by accident, that I needed a license to look after my patients.

A group of us from the museum had been studying the feeding habits of a clutch of hawks for several days. They were kestrels—falcons—which are really gorgeous birds. Some of the newborns already had their baby fuzz. When the parent birds were away looking for food, we'd climb up to inspect the nest, count the babies, and measure them. There were five of them. After observing the nest discreetly for hours every day, we became quite familiar with the kestrels' habits. If something were to go wrong, we would know it.

Nature maintains a strict, delicate balance between life and death. A female hawk lays her eggs over a period of days so that the hatching is staggered. She'll lay her first egg, and about three or four days later, she'll lay another, then another, until she's finished. Five eggs are typical for kestrels, and they start incubating immediately. The first bird to hatch will be a few days older than the next one, and so on down the line. These little ones have enormous appetites and couldn't possibly be fed enough to stay alive if they all hatched at the same time.

If the parent birds can bring enough grasshoppers and mice to the nest, the older babies share them with the younger ones, and everything is fine. But if there isn't enough food available, if the supply of grasshoppers and mice is down, the older babies will began to eat the younger ones. Like it or not, there is a certain amount of logic to nature's balancing act: If there isn't enough food, it's better to have fewer hawks so that at least some of them will make it to maturity and be able to reproduce. On the other hand, if the grasshoppers and mice are abundant, so are the hawks—unless something goes wrong.

The parent birds came often to the nest we were watching. They would feed their young and then tuck bits of food into the nest so the babies could continue to eat while the parents were looking for more. It was a good year for food, and we had every reason to expect the clutch to survive. Then the mother hawk was killed by a car. We could see that the father bird was exhausting himself trying to feed his hungry babies, but he just couldn't keep up with the demand. Since there wasn't enough food, the famished older babies began to cannibalize those who were newly hatched—it was the natural thing for them to do. One morning, when we climbed up to measure them, we found two dead babies, their heads bitten off. Only three were still alive. In a year where the food supply was down, we wouldn't have interfered. But this was supposed to be a good year for hawks.

I wanted to pull the nest and try to save what was left of the clutch. "Please!" I begged the man in charge of the project. "Let me take the nest home and hand-raise them! At least they'll have a chance."

He agreed with me that the nest was going to fail if we didn't do something. "Okay," he said. He phoned the museum for permission to pull the nest, and as soon as he got it, I headed for the tree.

"Wait a minute!" he called after me. "Do you have a license?"

"License?" I said. "To do what?"

"To keep hawks."

"Why do I need a license?"

"Because the state and federal governments say you do."

"That's crazy!"

Actually, it wasn't, as I learned when the reason for the ruling was explained to me. Hawks are birds of prey, and they're easy to train. In the wrong hands, they can become dangerous. Further, hawks fascinate people, and a lot of these magnificent birds would be kept in captivity if the government didn't discourage it.

That same day, I applied for a license from both the state and the federal Fish and Wildlife Departments; a state permit covers all kinds of wildlife, while federal permits apply only to birds. Prior to that day, I knew nothing about laws or licenses. I simply took care of baby bunnies, squirrels, raccoons, and an assortment of birds because it was what I wanted to do. If anyone had told me, "This is illegal," I would have said, "Well, too bad. I'll go where you can't find me, but I'm not going to stop what I'm doing."

Because I wanted to take the baby hawks home with

me right away, an inspector from the U.S. Fish and Wildlife Department came out to my home that afternoon to see what I was doing with my birds and animals. After watching me work with them, he issued me a license on the spot. "I almost don't know what to say," he said. "You know more about wildlife than any of us do." He explained that the license would cover my work with all my wild things. "This makes you a wildlife rehabilitator—officially," he said. I thanked him as I ran to my car. I wanted to get to that nest!

The three babies were alive and I brought them home. I felt honored—they were my first hawks. All three of them made it, and I released them back into their own world a few weeks later.

I enjoyed my volunteer work at the museum, but I knew I had to get a full-time job because we needed money. I also wanted to live closer to my mother. She used to babysit Debbie, Leah, and Sammy while I was watching kestrels for the museum project, and she offered to look after them if I got a job, but it was a long drive from her home to Edgewater Park in south Jersey where we lived. It made sense for us to move back to Pennsylvania. It was cheaper for us to live there, too. I gave the museum my notice and began looking for a house to rent in Bucks County. I found one in Langhorne. It was small, but all we could afford. "I wish we had more bedrooms," I told the girls. "We'll just have to double up."

Moving was nothing new to us. Sometimes a landlord who hadn't expected us to move in with such a menagerie asked us to leave, and sometimes our neighbors made life uncomfortable because they thought it was peculiar—"dirty," actually—for human beings to share their homes with wild things. When I told the girls about my decision, Leah's attitude was typical, "Oh, we're moving again?" she said. "Goody! New friends!" Debbie was more the loner, and I think it was harder for her, but she didn't object. Sammy, as the baby of the family, wasn't even consulted, but she let us know she didn't want to leave Edgewater Park.

"Can you get a job in Pennsylvania?" Debbie said.

"Something'll turn up," I assured her. I wasn't saying it just to make her feel good. I believed it.

One day, while I was packing boxes, I received a call from Julian Boryszewski, the director of the Churchville Outdoor Educational Center in Bucks County. He knew about my work from one of his staff members and had heard that I was moving to Pennsylvania. "We have an opening in our parks department," he said. "Can I interest you in it?"

I was flabbergasted. "I don't know," I told him. "What kind of a job?"

"We're looking for an assistant naturalist," he explained. "It's mostly educational work. You'd be working with various groups of people, teaching them about the environment."

"What kind of groups?"

"All kinds, the general public. Mostly kids and their parents—all kinds of kids, some with problems, some are poor, some are blind, some are in jail, some more fortunate, some live in the city, some in the country."

"I've never done anything like that."

"A lot of these kids don't know what a leaf is, let alone a tree," he said. "And some live in the middle of the woods and can't tell one tree from another. We try to give them a little introduction to the natural world. We take them out into the parks, show them around, try to answer their questions, let them see there's a world outside their own turf. I think you can handle it."

It sounded fascinating. The Churchville Outdoor Education Center was not far from the house I had rented. It was perfect! The only problem was my wild things.

"If you're interested," Julian said, "I'd like you to come out here and take a look at our place. Then we can talk some more."

"Oh, I'm *interested*!" I said. "Very!"

I went to Churchville later that week. After meeting the staff and learning more about the parks program, I knew I wanted the job. They were eager for me to begin. But there was still that one problem: Who would take care of my wild things?

"There's only one reason why I might not be able to do it," I said. "My animals—and my birds."

Julian looked completely puzzled, so I told him about my rehab work.

"I have to take care of the babies," I said. "I'd have to bring them with me."

"Here?"

"Yes, here. There's no other way. You see, they have to be fed almost every hour."

"I don't know how we can work that in," Julian said. "Animals aren't part of our program—we only do the parks."

"They wouldn't have to be involved in my work," I told him. "They just need to eat, and it doesn't take long to feed them. I'll make up the time."

We both were silent for a few seconds, but it seemed much longer. Then Julian said, "Well, I'm sure it will be all right for you to bring them with you. But you'll have to keep them out of sight."

Keeping them out of sight lasted for all of about five minutes. Every morning I'd arrive with my station wagon packed with boxes of baby skunks, raccoons, 'possums, and birds. I'd unload them and bring them into my office in the Churchville Outdoor Education Center, which was a fairly small room. I tried to keep them out of the way, but it was impossible. The windowsill was crammed with little boxes. They were all over the floor, and eventually they were in the hallway. I'd be talking to someone sitting across from my desk while a raccoon rambled around on my head and a 'possum peeked out of my pocket. I kept baby mice warm inside my blouse. Birds hopped all over my desk. Birdseed was everywhere.

Before I went home at the end of each day, I tried to

clean up. Still, I couldn't sweep up all the birdseed, and eventually it attracted the attention of some neighborhood rats. Well, rats are part of wildlife, too, and I could live with them. But my co-workers couldn't. There were screams, expressions of horror, and threats to poison them.

"No, please!" I said. "You can't poison them! That would be terrible!"

"Are you *defending* them?" one of the program directors said.

"I guess so," I said. "Yes—I *am*! Poison is cruel. And it's irresponsible. You might kill more than the rats—have you thought of that?"

I was getting somewhere. There was no more talk of rat poison. I didn't tell anyone that the biggest rat of all used to wait for me on my desk every morning. I'd open the door and there he'd be. He'd cock his head as if to say, "Well, how are you?" and he refused to budge until I gave him something to eat. He'd come back at lunchtime because he knew I brown-bagged it. I'd let him have some of my food at one end of my desk while I ate what was left at the other end. I tried to gobble mine before he finished his and moved in for more. In our own way, we got along.

Then I went on vacation, and when I returned there were no more rats. I noticed immediately that they were gone. I also noticed that the rest of the staff looked pretty sheepish and were avoiding me. It didn't take long to find out why: they had called in an exterminator while I was away.

"He didn't use poison!" Julian assured me. "It was done humanely."

"It's okay," I said. "I understand—I knew they were getting to be too much. But I'm glad you did it when I wasn't here, because I couldn't have gone along with it."

Except for feeding my patients, I didn't have to spend much time in my office. My boss was usually stuck with the paperwork and rarely got outdoors, but, as his assistant, I had the really neat job. I was outdoors all day, every day, teaching kids about the environment. That's what naturalists do—interpret the environment. I'd take groups of young people down to the pond or the lake, or for walks in the woods or the fields, and explain to them how all living things fit into the ecosystem. Sometimes I'd bring a few of my birds or animals along as part of the program. It was amazing how many of those young people had never been that close to anything wild, but once they were able to have the experience, and to understand a little bit about how another creature lived in the world, their own lives were changed. It changed the way they looked at a lot of other things in the world.

In the summer, when we went into the ghettos to conduct programs with groups of children, I'd take some baby birds and animals with me. It was an easy way to get the kids' attention, and I was comfortable talking about them.

Suburban ghettos are smaller than those in cities, but they're every bit as depressing. The worst one I saw was in a corner of an otherwise charming area in the eastern part of the county. I took two teenaged assistants with me and went looking for an old building where we were supposed to do an indoor program. When we arrived, we saw that the building had been almost completely destroyed by vandalism. It was in a black neighborhood, very poor and very hostile. Outside the door stood a husky young black teenager who glared at our car as we pulled up to the curb. My two assistants didn't want to get out, and I couldn't exactly blame them. The big fellow at the door seemed determined to keep us from entering. I couldn't exactly blame him, either. Who did we think we were, we white people dressed in our khaki shorts, sneakers, and ugly green T-shirts with the county emblem on them, coming to give the black kids a short talk about trees and flowers? We'd spend a couple of hours and then get out of there, feeling real good about ourselves, but the black kids had to stay.

When I got out of the car, I didn't see any small children around. A few more teen-aged boys were slouching along the building. Farther down the block were some boys who stood apart. I knew there were gangs in the area, and the two groups watched each other suspiciously. "You stay here," I told my two assistants, which was no problem because they had no intention of doing anything else.

As I walked up to the boy guarding the door, he took a step forward. He was trying to scare me and he succeeded. But then something else happened. When people try to push me around, they get my back up. Call it brave or stupid—and I suspect it bordered on stupidity—I thought to myself, "What can he do to me? Kill me? Well, I'm not afraid of death, so who cares what else he does?"

"Where are the children?" I asked him sharply.

He smiled at me as if I were the biggest fool he ever saw.

"We're here to work with the children, so go and get them!" I told him.

The smile left his face. He was angry.

"Get their mothers, too," I said. "Bring them all inside."

I turned back toward the car, and he muttered something crude to let me know he didn't think much of me. Turning around, I said, "So shut up and bring the children anyway!"

I began to unload the car, and when I looked around, the boy was gone. In a few minutes he came back with some children and a few mothers. They didn't seem to understand what was going on. Obviously our programs were not a regular event in the neighborhood.

"Open the door!" I told the boy. This time he did it without grumbling. He motioned the other boys to help us carry our boxes of animals into the building. The group down the street didn't join us. As we went inside, I said to my now-indispensable helper, "Ask your friends to keep an eye on those guys out there, will you? Don't let them bother us." He grinned and assigned two boys to stand outside.

The children were interested in the animals, but in that situation the animals were secondary. So was the whole program we conducted. What meant the most was that we were there, and that we were close enough to touch. Think about it: underprivileged children, especially black underprivileged children, can't just go up and touch a white person. It's something forbidden. Touching a white woman is particularly forbidden, and you sense it when you're with the children. I'd start by talking about the animals, and I'd be down on my knees so I could be on the children's level. I wanted to talk *with*, not *at*, them. I'd let the animals climb all over me as I talked, and the next thing I knew, the children would move closer. Then I'd feel a little finger touch my cheek—hesitantly. A hand would reach out and touch my hair—then withdraw. A hand would brush against my hand—lightly. The contacts were so uncertain. Then I'd hold out my hands, hoping they'd feel free to give me their hands, and when they did, I'd put their hands on the animals. If a child wanted to touch my hair and play with it the way they played with the animals, I'd say, "Okay, you can touch my hair if I can touch your hair." They could touch my face if I could touch their faces. The program stopped being a program; it became an exchange of touching.

The same thing happened with white children in ghettos. To touch a white adult female who was not from the ghetto was forbidden to them, so it was important for them to feel free to make contact with me. It breached part of the gap between us. When I saw some of them smile, I knew I was doing something that mattered. It was the kind of feedback we rarely get in this world.

Working with children came naturally to me, and I enjoyed that part of my job. The part I wanted to avoid was getting up in front of a group of people and giving a speech. The other staff members gave talks, and there

were a lot of requests for them, but our director knew
how I felt about it. "One of these days you'll have to do
it," he told me.

"One of these days" finally came along. Julian called
me into his office and told me I had to give a talk at
Neshaminy High School. He said he had agreed to do it,
but something came up.

"Oh, no!" I said. "Not me! That's a huge school—they
must have thousands of kids there!"

Julian tried to persuade me that speaking in public
would be a good experience for me. When that didn't
work, he threatened to fire me. "I told you it was part
of the job," he said.

"I have three children to support!" I said. I was so
angry I was afraid I would cry.

"And I have a program to run," he said.

I kept hoping it was a bad dream or a joke. When I
saw that he was quite serious, I considered killing him.
Then I faced reality. I needed the job. "Okay," I said.
"I'll do it. On one condition." I think he knew what was
coming. "I take my animals with me."

He smiled. "Good enough."

On the morning of the high school assembly, I was a
wreck. I had been up all night with a stomach ache and
diarrhea. I couldn't keep any food down. I was drenched
with sweat—thank God, I always wore an apron when I
handled the animals. Julian assigned a young staff member to go to the school with me, supposedly to help me
handle the boxes. (Actually I think Julian wanted him
there to push me out on the stage in case I froze at the
last minute.) I brought along a baby raccoon, a groundhog, a rabbit, and a great horned owl called Benjamin
who had a wing that wasn't repairable. Benjamin had a
name because he couldn't fly and was a permanent resident with us.

Neshaminy is a regional high school, with hundreds
of students. The auditorium is huge and the entire student body was there. I looked out at all those faces and

suddenly my mind went blank. If you had asked me my name, I couldn't have told you. I couldn't remember why I was there or what I was supposed to say. The only friends I had in the world were the wild ones in the boxes arranged on a long table in the middle of the stage. As I heard the principal introducing me, I held out my arm to Benjamin and he perched on it.

I felt my heart pounding all over my body, and my throat was bone-dry. Not a sound came from the audience, and I couldn't bring myself to look out there. To compose myself I began to talk to Benjamin, just as I always did. Then it seemed only natural to start telling the audience who he was and how he came to be there. By then I was looking out at the kids and not even realizing it. I felt as if I were down on my knees on the floor, talking to a group of children.

I don't remember a word I said that morning, but when I finished and heard the applause, I could see that I had completely captured my audience's attention. I was *thrilled*! I had no idea what I did, but I've been doing it ever since. Now, if you put a microphone in front of me, you can't shut me up.

After that, my nervousness disappeared, and I did my share of speaking. Of course, the birds and animals always stole the show. Very often someone—a student, a teacher, a businessperson—would ask me how to get into wildlife rehabilitation.

Anytime I work with children I hope I can reach at least one of them with the message that I care about them. If they can see that I give of my time and my life to make a difference in the wild world—and that I'm trying to make a difference in their world—then that means I did something that day. Everybody says, "What can *I* do?" Well, if all the *I*'s did something, everybody would be doing something. We could change this planet. One person *can* make a difference. If you do something in your own life, it makes a difference in someone else's life.

Julian was so pleased with his success in forcing me to speak in public that he decided it was time for me to go on television. The opportunity came along when Bob Mercer, director of the Silver Lake Nature Center, was unable to take part in a panel discussion of environmental problems on a closed-circuit TV channel in Levittown. He asked me to fill in for him.

"Sure," I said, knowing how surprised Julian would be when he heard that I didn't try to get out of it. "When?"

The show was scheduled for the afternoon of a day when I was conducting a morning program for a group of children. I saw no reason to cancel the program. "I'll have enough time," I told Bob Mercer. After all, what else did I have to do except drive from one location to another? And my animals would be with me.

I had forgotten how dirty I got doing those programs. Ghettos, whether they're in a city or the rolling hills of suburbia, are dirty places. And the children who live there can't help but get dirty. When they touch you, you get dirty, too. I didn't mind. It was the way the kids and I told each other we cared. By some people's standards my animals weren't so clean, either. When they had to defecate or urinate, they did it, even if they happened to be climbing all over me. I was used to it, but that's also why I wore an apron when I worked with them—I could whip it off and look almost neat whenever visitors came around.

On the day of the TV show, my children's program ran a little long. It was the middle of July, and both the temperature and the humidity were in the nineties. I was dirty, hot, and exhausted, so I decided to drive back to Merce's office in the Silver Lake Nature Center and wash up before going to the TV studio. In my hurry, I completely forgot that a baby 'possum was sleeping in my hair.

In those days I wore my hair very long, almost down to my waist. It was thick and heavy, and animals loved to play with it. To show the children how a mother 'possum carries her young ones around on her back, I had put a baby in my hair so the children could see how it clung to me. It was extremely small, and had disappeared in my hair. After a while I didn't even feel it, especially when it settled down and fell asleep.

When I walked into the center, Bob Mercer got very upset. "What are you doing here?" he asked me. "You're supposed to go on TV in less than an hour!"

"Please," I said, "I've got to get some sleep."

"Sleep?" he exploded. "There's no time to sleep!"

"I only need a few minutes," I assured him.

He let me use his office and I curled up in a corner on the floor. I was so tired I fell asleep immediately. And almost immediately Merce was waking me up. "It's time to leave," he said gently. "I'm sorry, but it's time now."

He helped me up and walked with me toward the front door. "Wait," I said, as I began to realize what was happening. "At least let me wash my face and hands. I'm filthy."

"No time," he said. "This is a live show—you can't be late."

"But, Merce, I'm filthy! Really filthy!"

"Don't worry—the lights are very bright. They'll make you look clean." I think he would have said anything to get me out of there.

I arrived on the TV set seconds before the show began. I took my seat among the other panelists and decided not to worry about how I looked. My birds and animals were with me, like a security blanket.

Merce was right about the lights: they were blinding. And hot. Hot enough, in fact, to awaken a sleeping baby 'possum. When I felt it stirring, I suddenly remembered it was there. Instinctively my hand went toward my head, but the theme music began playing. We were on! "Oh, well," I said to myself and dropped my hand.

Unfortunately, 'possums are like all other babies when they wake up—they empty their bowels and bladders— and the next thing I knew, something wet and hot slid down the side of my face. What a way to break into the media!

After working with children, where you never know what's going to happen next, I was used to winging it. Part of me was dying of embarrassment, but another part realized I had to make the best of the situation. I reached up, disentangled the 'possum from my hair, let the camera get a good look at it, and began to explain what it was doing there. That turned out to be a neat way to describe the parks programs—with a few laughs thrown in.

During the next few years I taxied an increasing number of little boxes back and forth between my home and my office in Churchville. Gradually, it became obvious that I had to choose between being a naturalist and being a rehabber because there wasn't enough time to be both. By then Debbie, Leah, and Sammy were in school during the day, which left me free to concentrate on my job. But once the girls came home, I wanted to be there for them. They were the most important part of my life, and I wanted to enjoy them as much as possible before they went off on their own. Mothering, rehabbing, working— in that order—were essential to my existence, but it was becoming harder and harder to juggle them. The problem was that I needed money, and I couldn't earn it as a wildlife rehabilitator. Yet I couldn't give up working with my wild things.

One day in the fall of 1974, I went to look at a hawk in Newtown, a lovely semi-rural community in the eastern part of Bucks County. The man who was keeping the hawk had a proper license to do so, but he and his wife were planning to move to another state and he wasn't sure he could take the hawk with him. To move a hawk out of one state and into another, he needed several kinds of state and federal permits. He also had to provide proper facilities for the hawk in the new state before he brought the bird in. He wasn't sure he would have all the paperwork completed before it was time for him to move, and he was looking for someone to take care of his hawk in case he had to leave it behind temporarily. Somebody he knew had heard about me, and he called to ask me if I would look after the hawk. I said I would and made an appointment to meet him at his home.

The house where the hawk and its keepers lived was set far back from a country road in the midst of acres and acres of fields and woods. As I drove down the long, puddled drive, I began to remember how I felt as a child, having so much natural space around me. I choked up a little. The house was large and very old. Once it had been a gracious old farmhouse, but now it was in sorry need of major repairs. There were a few outbuildings that weren't being used for anything I could see. The grass, the shrubbery, the trees—everything was overgrown, as if no one cared. I hated to see that happen to a house.

I parked at the rear door, where the driveway ended. The man came out and showed me into the kitchen, which was a plain, institutional-looking room. There were cupboards and the necessary appliances, but nothing that said this was a home.

We sat down at a small table and talked about hawks. When he seemed satisfied that I was capable of looking after the bird, we went outside to take a look at it. It was in a proper weathering pen, designed to protect hawks when they sit out in the sun and rain as they like to do. It was a circular pen framed in wood and covered on all sides and the top with wire screening so that the hawk couldn't get out and another hawk couldn't get in to attack it. The hawk was tethered by a leather lead to a ring perch in the center of the pen, which gave it enough room to fly and move about without hitting the wire screening and damaging its feathers. The ring itself had X-shaped crossbars to prevent the bird from flying through the ring and getting its lead tangled in it.

When we went back into the kitchen for a cup of coffee, I tried to look into the other rooms, but they were too dark for me to see anything. I asked the man what he and his wife were going to do with the house.

"It's not ours," he said. "We rent it. We've been here about two years, and I really hate to leave it."

"Who owns it?"

"The Archdiocese of Philadelphia," he said. "They've been so nice to us, and the rent is real low."

"Do they have another tenant?"

"No, and I'm sorry about that. I don't like to leave the house empty. But the diocese doesn't seem concerned about that—I think they plan to bulldoze it down and use the land for something else."

"Oh, they can't!" I said. "It's too lovely here!"

"Well," he said, "it needs a lot done to it. The owners aren't interested in keeping it up because they don't plan to hold onto it. That's why the rent is so cheap."

When he told me what the rent was, my whole life began rearranging itself without my consent. The rent was less than I was paying. Although I had seen only the kitchen, I knew from the outside that the house was much bigger than the one where the girls and I were living. It would be wonderful if Debbie, Leah, and Sammy could have their own rooms. And I knew I would be happy there. I had grown up in big, old houses that had some history to them.

And all the space! The outbuildings would be perfect for some of my wild babies. For those that weren't yet able to go back outdoors, there was plenty of room for a nursery in the house. The neighbors weren't even close enough to see. We could build more pens for the birds of prey. Maybe—maybe—I could start a wildlife rehabilitation center here. Maybe I could rehab fulltime. Maybe the center could become a foundation for children of the wild. I could go out and raise money for it. Hell, I could go on TV and talk in high schools and to anybody who would listen!

"I want it!" I said.

The man looked pleased. "Gee, I'd really like to see someone living here," he said. "It's a good old house—at least it could be, with some work."

"If they'll keep the rent low, we'll fix it up," I told him. "How many bedrooms are there?"

"Four," he said. "But only two are usable. The two on the third floor are closed off—the bathroom doesn't work up there and the whole floor's a mess."

I took a deep breath and asked him for the number of someone I should call. I wanted a decision right away. He called the real estate agent who handled the property and put me on the phone. Within a few minutes I had given the agent all the information he needed. He said he'd call the diocese and get back to me shortly.

While we waited I took a tour of the rest of the house. It was grim. The walls of the living room were dark red. The draperies were dark red, too. The windows were covered by overgrown shrubbery, and hardly any light made its way inside. Upstairs the rooms were in pitiful condition, with paint peeling and woodwork scarred. The one working bathroom wouldn't work much longer, I was certain of that; it would have to be completely replaced. The third floor was horrendous.

But—the house had been built to embrace a family. Its large fireplaces, deep windowsills, and charming nooks were places where you could sit and talk, or sit alone and dream. It was a house you wanted to *be* in. I could feel that people long gone had been happy there. It was exactly where I wanted my daughters to grow up.

We have a lot of work ahead of us, I thought. We'd start by letting the light in. Then we'd keep it in by painting the walls in light colors. It would take zillions of coats, but I didn't care. I already knew where the wildlife nursery would be, but I'd have to find a way to supply it with incubators and more sophisticated medicines.

Then I realized that the landlords hadn't said yes yet. And would they give up their plans to demolish the house? This was not a temporary residence for us. I wanted us to move in for good. I decided it was too soon to confront that particular problem.

The broker called back and said the house was mine. He asked me to stop by his office and sign the necessary papers on my way home. I was there in minutes.

It was hard for the girls to believe what I was telling them that night. There were so many details, so many ifs, so many enormous changes that were about to happen to all of us. But I like change. It's a natural, exciting part of life, and I have always welcomed it.

"Tell me about the house again," Sammy said.

"Well," I said, pulling her close to me, "there's something extra special about it."

"Like what?" she wanted to know.

"Like—it was meant to be. Like it was meant to be *for me*. As if it was waiting there for me to come and find it."

Sammy was having a little trouble following me. "It's a gift, Sammy," I said. Then she understood.

What I didn't tell her was that I was holding my breath when I accepted it.

3 / Raccoons in the Bed

It's late October. As far as baby birds are concerned, the fledgling tree is closed down for the winter. But now some baby 'coons have moved into its branches. If you want to see them, you have to know what to look for. Better yet, walk outside with me and stand under the tree while we talk. Almost immediately you will hear some activity in the tree's upper branches, and suddenly—plop!—a young raccoon will come tumbling out of the tree to land near your feet. Plop!—another will follow, and then another, until all five are rolling around, cuffing each other, and—if you let them—scurrying up your legs, onto your shoulders, even onto your head and into your hair.

But you must not let them do that. And I won't invite you to walk outside and stand under the tree with me. Not anymore. The high incidence of rabies in raccoons during the past several years makes contact with them too dangerous.

Raccoons used to be the biggest part of my practice. Now I have to turn most of them away, and those I do take in, I often put down. It's especially hard to do that to babies that look healthy, but we can't take the chance that they might be infected. Releasing them is another problem. During the summer, with so many people and cars coming and going, we can't possibly release the 'coons here. They might get into a car and bite someone. Or someone might walk by a 'coon, not see it, and accidentally step on it. If that were to happen, the animal would bite. So we have to release our raccoons somewhere else. Unfortunately, we release only a few now because animals can carry rabies for a long time before the symptoms show up, and we can't risk sending a "hot" raccoon back into the wild.

Baby 'coons need so much handling. We bottlefeed them every four hours; then we burp them and potty them, so there's a lot of contact. And a raccoon is different from other animals in that it has a very wet mouth. When a baby nurses, it blows bubbles and slobbers constantly, and its saliva gets on your hands. If you should happen to have the tiniest scratch on your hands—even one you haven't noticed—and if the animal is infected, then you could become infected, too. But it's easy to forget about the danger when the creature you're feeding is so darling! It's sucking on the bottle, sucking your hands, crawling all over you, nibbling on your ears, poking its tiny paws into your mouth, and nuzzling into your neck because it's soft and warm there.

Skunks also have a high incidence of rabies—in some areas it's worse than in raccoons—but their mouths are drier. Their habits are different, too. Skunk babies will follow you around and they're very playful, but they don't lick you. And once they grow up, you don't want to get near them. So I tend not to worry about rabies in skunks.

In the nursery, we try to take some extra precautions when we handle raccoons. When our patient load increases early in spring, I tell my staff and volunteers to wear gloves. "If I see you without gloves on, I'll fire you," I tell them. But if I followed through on my threat,

I'd have to fire myself because I'm the worst—and usually the first—offender. After a few weeks I get so busy and tired that I forget to be careful. If I'm working with baby raccoons that have been here for a while, I don't even think of gloves. I know that's wrong. Rabies kills.

If you could take a human baby, a puppy, a kitten, and a monkey, and put them all together—you'd know how God made raccoons. Put all that delight, all that mischief, agility, intelligence, curiosity, and affection in one little package, stick a mask on it, and you've got a raccoon. I don't know anyone who can stand within arm's length of a baby 'coon and not want to nuzzle it.

It's hard for me to cut raccoons out of my life. I love the soft fuzziness of them. And I remember them as friends of the family. They were my children's best buddies.

Then we didn't even think about rabies, and we handled baby 'coons too much. We didn't realize until much later that it wasn't necessary, or even helpful, to treat them like pets. We kept them too long, until the animals themselves had to let us know it was time for them to go. Adult raccoons are another story because they haven't been conditioned to trust people. Usually they're brought in injured or sick, and they're not about to let us put our hands on them. We have to anesthetize them to treat their wounds, and we put their medicine in their food. As soon as they recover, they're ready to leave, and we don't try to stop them.

We always had more babies than adults. People would cut down a big old tree and find a nest of coons in it. Or they'd bring in a nest of babies after the mother was killed on the road. If the babies were very young, we'd put them in one of our isolettes, and as soon as they didn't need that moist heat we'd transfer them to a box. When we lived in Langhorne, and until recently even here, my office and nursery were in the house, so everywhere you looked there were boxes of coons. As soon as they were old enough to climb out of the boxes, they were constantly underfoot, just like kittens or puppies. I had cages where I could put them when they got to be a nuisance, and to keep them out of harm's way—or mine—but I didn't use cages much. Most of the time the 'coons had the run of our house, and I mean that literally: they were into everything. But I don't like to keep animals in cages, and I do it as little as possible. Wild things need to be free, and we didn't mind sharing our lives with them. Not everyone agreed. One of the reasons why we moved so often before we came to Newtown was that some of our neighbors, and many of my children's friends, thought it was weird for human beings to have such close relationships with animals. To us it was normal. My daughters will tell you that in our family the animals came first, and at times it was a cause for resentment. But that was the way we lived.

When my daughters came home from school, they played with raccoons more often than they played with other children. It was an excellent way for them to get an education in the ways of wildlife and have fun at the same time. Naturally, the animals were learning about us, too. At night, after the girls went to sleep, the 'coon babies would creep upstairs and curl up in bed with them. When I went to wake the children in the morning, I always found at least one baby raccoon in each bed, and as soon as they woke up it was playtime again. Downstairs we'd be stepping over them in the kitchen while we made breakfast, and when we sat down to our Cheerios, there they were on the table, reaching their incredible fingers into our bowls and helping themselves. We had to eat fast to get our share. After the girls left for school and I went upstairs to make the beds, I often found a warm, furry lump under the covers—a 'coon, sleeping in.

With our friends, it was "Love us, love our 'coons," because 'coons found their way into our social life as well. While some people found that a pleasure, others found it a reason to give up seeing us. Occasionally we had an embarrassing moment when a 'coon chose to indulge in a favorite pastime: masturbation. Raccoons do it frequently, and we were accustomed to it. When my daughters first asked me what "the coon was doing," I had to think about it for a moment. I couldn't give a single answer that would suit each girl's age and understanding of sex, because they were four years apart—a big difference. So I said, "He's playing with his belly button," which was only slightly off target because a 'coon's penis is close to his belly button. However, from that moment on, whenever a male 'coon rolled back on his haunches and began to masturbate in front of our guests, Debbie, Leah, and Sammy, in perfect tour-guide fashion, would announce, "See? He's playing with his belly button!"

On some mornings we came downstairs and found our young 'coons asleep in a wing chair or a corner of the sofa. That warned us what we could expect to find in the kitchen: cabinets open and boxes of cereal thrown to the floor and pulled apart in search of goodies. We soon learned not to keep our cookies in the cabinet over the sink because the height of the cabinet was no match for the ingenuity of a coon. Using the drawer handles as steps, they would climb up, open the cabinet doors with their handlike front paws, throw the bags of cookies down on the floor, and have a feast. With so much food in their bellies, it's no wonder they slept in the living room; they couldn't make it up to the girls' bedrooms on the third floor.

Raccoons are nocturnal creatures, and as soon as the babies were old enough to go outside, we'd take them out in their cages and leave the cage doors open for them to come and go as they pleased. Of course, we kept feeding them because they hadn't learned to feed themselves yet. The idea was to give them a sense of freedom by releasing them gradually.

It was up to us to take the role of their mother and teach them about the 'coon's world. So, every evening, when darkness was beginning to come on, the girls and I used to walk down to the creek with five or six raccoons scampering after us, as they would have done with their mother. We'd kick stones into the water, and the 'coons would go in after them. 'Coons love the water and they love to play, so it was a very splashy time for all of us. We'd wade into the creek, knowing they would follow us. Then we'd reach down to the creek bottom, groping for crayfish and bugs that 'coons love to eat—and pretty soon the little ones were digging for their own. For them it was a lesson in self-sufficiency. For us it was a magical time in a world few people ever get to enter.

We wanted to make their transition back to the wild as gentle as possible—for them as well as for us—so while they were busy splashing and eating, we'd leave quietly and head for home. At first they'd follow us straight back to the house, but gradually they began to stay longer at the creek. They had things to do, and nighttime was their time to do them. Besides, they knew how to come home when they were ready. We left their cages outside so they would have warm, dry, secure places to sleep in, but eventually they gave them up in favor of beds of their own choosing. They were getting comfortable out there in the woods—and that's what we wanted for them.

But they were not quite ready to leave. Sometimes, just before dawn, they would find their way back into our house. A few of our bedroom windows are only inches above the slope of the kitchen roof or across from the branch of a big tree next to the house—a situation made to order for raccoons. It was the easiest thing in the world for them to jump up from the kitchen roof or across from the tree and land on a windowsill. The next easiest thing was to tear a hole in the screen and go inside. After playing all night in the swamp, they were usually full of mud, which didn't bother them in the least as they climbed into various beds. In the morning, when I looked in, I'd find mud everywhere, and 'coons in their typical snuggling position: draped around the girls' heads. I don't know how the girls put up with it, but I always found them sleeping comfortably in spite of muddy 'coon feet resting on their faces and muddy 'coon fingers poking into their noses and mouths. "It's how they play," Debbie explained to Sammy, who was not always as tolerant as her older sisters. "They just fall asleep playing."

Raccoons aren't the only animals that know where our bedroom windows are. The word gets around. Young owls that we've released will sometimes come back and sit outside my window, bumping their heads against the screen until they tear a hole in it. Then suddenly, there they are, screeching their baby cheers at me until I get up and give them something to eat. Sometimes they aren't looking for food, just attention. But we always know that if it is warm enough for us to leave a window open, we will have screens to repair and raccoons in our beds. Or—in our bacon grease.

I have to take the blame for the bacon grease episode, although at the time it happened I wasn't feeling the least bit noble. It was summer and the day had been a long one filled with emergencies and frequent feedings. The isolettes were packed with babies, and every box and cage had a patient in it. I had been up very late, and I was too tired to cope with the bacon fat left over from our dinner. Usually I put it in a container, let it congeal, and feed it to the birds the next morning, but that night I was falling asleep on my feet. Debbie had been helping me, and she was tired, too. "This can wait till morning," I said, pushing the pan of drippings toward the back of the stove. Debbie's smile of relief was interrupted by a yawn, and mine followed immediately. We laughed. "Let's go," I said. I hugged her to me as we walked together through the dining room toward the staircase in the living room.

My bedroom is on the second floor. " 'Night, honey," I said, kissing her lightly on the forehead (because she was at that early teen age when mother-kisses are not always welcome).

" 'Night, Mom," she said drowsily. I watched her climb the stairs to the third floor, her thick, curly red hair rising and falling with the slow movement of her shoulders. I realized how late it was—past midnight. Debbie had to go to school the next day. I shouldn't have allowed her to stay up so late, but when I'm working with animals I forget about time. That's all right if it's only me working with them. But I remembered that from the moment Debbie came home from school that afternoon, she had been working with me every minute. She never asked what had to be done. She did it. And she did it well. When she worked with me, she was so much a part of me that sometimes I forgot she was there. You can't do that to people. I was sorry.

"Debbie," I called softly. She was at the top of the stairs, and I didn't want to wake Leah and Sammy. I could barely see her face. In fact I could only see to the middle of her nose. The rest was in darkness.

"Thanks," I said. I really wanted to run up the stairs and hug her, but I was too tired and she was too much a teenager.

I saw her head tilt to one side. "What for?" she said.

"For being such a big help."

"It's okay."

"Deb?"

"Yeah?"

"Thanks—for being you. Good night." I turned and went into my bedroom. I closed the door. A few seconds passed, and then I heard Debbie's footsteps going toward her room.

That night I was too tired to hear anything. I got up for the 3:00 A.M. feeding in the nursery, and after I finished I fell asleep quickly, which was unusual for me.

The next morning, when I went upstairs to wake the girls, I thought some of the stairs felt a bit gummy under my sneakers. I promised myself I'd look at them more closely later, when I had time. A screen in Leah's room was torn open, so I was not surprised to find a raccoon in her bed. But I was horrified at what else I saw. Both Leah and the 'coon were sleeping contentedly, and both of them were covered with some kind of grease! The 'coon's fur was matted. Leah's doll-like features were streaked with grease—it was in her nose, her eyes, her mouth, and all over her cheeks. Her pale blond hair was sticky with it. *Bacon* grease!

I hurried to Debbie's room and then to Sammy's, noticing with each footstep that the hallway floor felt just like the steps—gummy! Both girls were asleep, and their heads were covered with bacon grease. But there were no raccoons in their beds. Apparently all the damage had been done by one intruder, who had left a gummy trail. I followed it downstairs, through the living room, the dining room, and into the kitchen. There I found a scene that made me want to leave by the nearest door. This was where the 'coon must have begun his adventure after he came in the bedroom window. He had immersed himself in the pan of congealed drippings and then, covered with grease, gone on to paint my entire kitchen. Gooey streaks of grease were all over the cabinets, the counters, the floor, the windows, the table, the chairs, the walls—as high up as he could reach!

I was wondering where and how to begin to clean up the mess, when I heard the first outcry from the third floor. "Mom-m-m!" It sounded like Leah.

This was no time for me to be anything but absolutely calm. "I know," I called. "Head for the shower!" Somehow I managed to get the girls out of the house in time to catch the school bus. They had to gulp down their cereal, and their hair was wet and still a little sticky, but by then we were beginning to laugh at the disaster. "It's Mortimer," Leah insisted, referring to the 'coon in her bed. She didn't agree with me that we shouldn't name our animals. "He just loves to plague me!" I had the feeling she was somewhat pleased to be singled out for such attention.

As soon as I fed the babies in the nursery, I went upstairs to change the sheets. And there, in Leah's bed, totally oblivious to the fact that it would take me the rest of the day, or more, to clean up the mess he had made, was a great, big, greasy raccoon, sound asleep. When I woke him up by pulling at the sheet, he waddled groggily downstairs to the back door, leaving another gooey trail behind him.

I recognized him, and it was indeed the 'coon Leah called Mortimer. We usually can't tell one 'coon from another once they grow up, but this one had always been memorable because of his size. He was very young when someone brought him in with several other babies in a nest that had been knocked out of a tree struck by lightning during a storm. He was big for his age then, and he grew up to be the biggest raccoon I have ever seen. At four months, he weighed about thirty pounds.

"He's too fat," Leah said.

"All he does is sleep all day and eat," Debbie said. "We spoil him too much."

We were always going to put Mortimer on a diet, but we never did. He was too lovable—and we knew we wouldn't have him for long. We told ourselves that once he got back into the wild, he would shape up. Those were the days when we held onto our babies too long and allowed them to share too much of our human lives. But eventually even Mortimer stopped coming back to sleep in our beds. When we didn't see him for over a month, we assumed that he was resuming a normal raccoon lifestyle.

Then, one warm evening late in the fall, I woke up hearing strange noises. I sat up and listened. One of my windows was open, but there were no owls, no raccoons tearing at the screen. The sound came from outside, somewhere below my bedroom. It was a shuffling, scratching noise, and it seemed to be coming from the back door, near the kitchen.

I got up and went downstairs. I stood by the back door and listened. The sound started again, insistently. Something was scratching at the door. I opened it cautiously, ready to slam it shut if I had to—and there at my feet, in the soft light from the moon, I saw this very large—huge!—raccoon. He sat back on his heinie the way 'coons do, looking pear-shaped, and I could hear from the snorty sound of his breathing that he had a bad cold. He was sniffly and gooky with mucous, and he had come to the one place where he knew he could get help—his mom's back door.

I held out my arms to him and he reached up to me. "Mortimer, I think it's you," I said as I picked him up. "Is it? Really?" You always have to wonder. But when I put my arms down to an animal and talk to it, if it responds in an unnatural manner, such as reaching up to *me*, then it *has* to know me. Normally a wild animal would never wander out of the woods and reach up to me. It has to be one I've held and nursed, one who's used to being in my arms. And this was a coon of Mortimer's size.

"You poor baby, you're a mess," I murmured to him as I gathered him up in my arms. He was like a sick kid, pushing his head down into my neck and hanging onto me. I brought him into the nursery and gave him a baby aspirin and a decongestant with no trouble at all, another sign that this was a former patient. I used a baby's nasal aspirator to suck the mucous out of his nostrils and got him to the point where he could breathe more easily. By then it was time for my 3:00 A.M. feeding, which took longer than usual because I had to keep stopping to pick up Mortimer and hold him. The aspirin had made him too drowsy to sit up by himself and unless he was sitting up, he had difficulty breathing.

When it was time for me to go back to bed, I wondered, *"Now* what can I do with him?" The minute I laid him down, he couldn't breathe. When I held him, he improved. I wanted to get some nourishment into him, but decided against milk because he was beyond the age for nursing. I decided that apple juice might do it. I offered him some in a bottle, and he sucked on it, more proof that this was definitely one of my own.

I considered sitting up with him for what was left of the night, but finally I decided that was silly. I carried him upstairs to my bed and propped him up against some pillows so that he was in a sitting position. He didn't object. Besides being sick, he was very tired and just wanted to snuggle and sleep. I wanted to be sure he didn't fall over on his side while he slept, so I climbed into bed next to him and put one arm over him, exactly as I would have done with a sick child.

When I got up in the morning he was still asleep. He looked so comfortable, I decided to let him stay in bed for a while. He stayed for three days. For some of that time I carried him around in my arms as I did my work, because he was still badly congested. At night he slept in my bed. His infection was clearing up, but he was exhausted from it.

There is a point in a wild animal's recovery when it has had enough of human company. In spite of all the care and nurture it may be getting, it responds to its instincts and seeks its own kind. Well, let me tell you, the same thing happens to human beings. Reaching down to a sick raccoon, and then having him reach up to me, was a lovely experience. Seeing him respond to my care was beautiful. But by the second day of his confinement, I began to think, "What am I going to do with this animal? Look at him—comfy, comfy, in *my* bed, letting me bring him food and apple juice, nuzzling my neck while I carry all thirty pounds of him around until my arms are sore and stiff."

I slapped at the back of my neck. "Besides, I've got fleas!" The novelty was wearing off, and my good intentions were very thin.

Leah said it for me: "Is he ever going to move on?"

Then, on the third night, he woke me up by moving off the pillows.

"Mortimer? You okay?" I had given in to calling him by name.

He jumped off the bed and scampered toward the window over the kitchen roof. It was open. Up on the sill, he swiped at the screen with those sharp claws and tore a ragged hole in it. He looked back at me for a second as if to say, "Thanks, Mom—see ya," and then he was gone. It was typical of the lovely way wild things will often end a relationship that, however beautiful, could never last.

We never saw Mortimer again. At least, not that we know of.

A few years ago, when the threat of rabies in raccoons became so alarming, we stopped admitting any 'coons at all. I couldn't risk the lives of my staff and our many visitors. But it was a difficult year for all of us. And, as anyone who knows me can tell you, I don't tolerate defeat very well. All you have to do is tell me I can't do something, and I'll find a way to do it.

It was an incident involving one of my volunteers that convinced me to look for a way to treat at least some raccoons. Diane Nickerson had been an answer to a prayer. She knew nothing about wildlife rehabilitation when she first began to work at The Aark, but she learned fast and had the right combination of concern, dedication, and tough-mindedness that allows a person to care without being overcome by sentimentality. For a while she was one of our foster parents, and when she accidentally killed a baby rabbit by inserting a feeding tube into its lung instead of its stomach—which is easy to do—she was overcome with grief.

"Please, don't ever ask me to do that again!" she said. She couldn't talk about it without crying.

"Okay," I told her, "but look at it this way. If you try

to feed a baby rabbit that can't feed itself, you might make a mistake and kill it. You're new at this, and that's a chance you have to take. But if you don't feed that rabbit, it's going to die, for sure."

When Diane went home that day, she took another baby rabbit with her. I knew how scared she must have been, but she inserted the tube properly and the rabbit survived. When it was old enough to be released, Diane took on another baby. I admire that kind of courage—it's hard to find.

Diane eventually became a volunteer. She was in the nursery when a woman brought in two baby 'coons she had found on her property. She said she hadn't seen any sign of the mother. Diane told her we couldn't accept any raccoons, but when the woman said she didn't know what else to do with them, Diane relented. She told the woman we would take them, but we would have to put them down. The woman agreed to that and left.

I walked into the nursery shortly after Diane euthanized the babies. She didn't look up or say a word as she went about checking the isolettes and cages.

"What happened?" I asked her.

She started to tubefeed a baby 'possum, and I could see she was trying to get control of herself. Finally she said, very matter-of-factly, "A woman came in with two little 'coons. They were so healthy. I couldn't see anything wrong with them. All they needed was someone to mother them. And I wasn't able to do that."

Diane looked up at me and her eyes were filled with tears, but she wasn't going to let them spill over. "I did what you told me to do," she said. "I put them down."

I could feel her pain. I put my arm around her shoulder.

"I apologized to them first," she said. "I always do that when I put something down—but especially to these two."

I lifted a baby skunk out of an isolette and used my foot to pull over a straight-backed chair so I could sit down next to Diane. The skunk was so tiny I could hold it in one hand while I coaxed it to open its mouth to the nipple of a small bottle. For a while Diane and I concentrated on our patients. There was only the irregular sucking sound of helpless creatures trying to adjust to instruments that were totally alien to them.

Then Diane said, "Can't we do something?"

"I don't know—but I'm thinking."

"Can't we give them rabies shots?"

"They haven't developed a vaccine that works for wildlife."

"Why not?" Diane said.

"Because there's no money in it." This is one of the harsh realities of rehabbing. Protecting wild things costs money, lots of it, but it just doesn't turn a buck. Our world will be a better place if we learn how to protect raccoons from rabies—but it won't be a richer place. I'll also admit that raccoons certainly aren't an endangered species. In fact, there are too many of them for the little bit of habitat that's left. But we're the ones who took their habitat away from them, and we ought to be able to help them now that they're in trouble. Look at it this way: if we didn't crowd them into less and less space, if we didn't force them to look for food in our city sewers, our trash cans, and our backyards, they wouldn't be so susceptible to rabies. And neither would we.

We don't know whether the rabies vaccines used for domestic animals will work for wildlife because nobody has put up enough money to conduct experiments that will give us some answers. We know that the existing vaccines work some of the time, but we can't be sure how much of the time. We don't know how different species might react to them. If we did know, if we did develop a vaccine that really worked for wild animals, who would buy the product, aside from a few rehabbers who might not be able to scrape up enough money for it? And if you can't sell a product, where's the incentive to develop it?

I was doing my silent soapbox routine, saying all the things in my mind that I had often said out loud. When I was younger I was very outspoken, and it had gotten me nowhere. I still speak up, but my timing is getting better. Now I wait until I have an interested audience, and I stop when I see that I'm asking more of them than they want to give. If I can't get their support, that's okay. I go my own way.

My little skunk was ready to go back to its isolette. As I lifted it carefully into the enclosure and reached for another baby, I started thinking out loud. "Maybe we can take in a few 'coons."

I waited until fall, when we had only a few patients coming in each day and hardly any volunteers. I called my staff together—by that time Diane was one of them—and told them how I felt. "I don't know about you, but this past summer drove me crazy," I said. "I don't want to stop working with raccoons, but I don't want to get rabies. I don't want you to get it, either.

"Personally I'm willing to take a few risks. I'm not asking you to do the same. You'll have to make your own decision."

Then I explained what I thought our policy might be. We would treat injured adult raccoons. If someone brought in a raccoon that was hit by a car and we thought we could save it, we would take it in because an adult 'coon can be treated without direct physical contact. We would anesthetize the animal, suture it up, isolate it in a cage by itself, give it medication, and release it immediately on recovery. The cage, of course, would have to be sterilized before we put another patient in it. Better yet, we would use certain cages only for raccoons.

"We'll even keep our raccoons in a section by themselves," I said.

"What about the babies?" Diane asked.

"We can't take more than a few," I told her. Babies, because they have to be bottlefed, require handling, and lots of it, so the risks are greater.

"We'll have to get some family history when someone brings us baby 'coons. If they come from a nest in a chimney—I'm willing to take a chance with them. If it's a baby from a healthy family nest that was evicted from an attic by an exterminator, I'll take it. But I'll wear gloves, I promise. At all times."

We can't be sure that a healthy-looking baby isn't infected. Some scientists think 'coons can be infected in the mother's womb if the mother has rabies and is in the "shedding," or contagious, stage. Or, an infected mother can infect a baby by biting through an umbilical cord. Nevertheless, I felt that if we took the precaution of learning something about the animal's family history, we could reduce our risks.

For instance, suppose people brought in a baby 'coon they found at the base of a tree that they knew sheltered a 'coon family. The mother wasn't anywhere in sight, so the people assume she must have been hit by a car and killed. But they're not sure. Since they haven't seen her, they can't observe any instability in her behavior. In that case, I would have to think, "Wait a minute—if the mother has rabies, and she's really in the throes of it, then she's not able to take care of her babies. She's too sick. So the babies will peel out of the nest looking for food and care. Or, maybe the mother is still able to take some care of them and she tries to keep them clean, as animal mothers always do. Suppose a baby has been playing with his siblings and one of them scratched him. Just a tiny nick. But with a mother 'coon licking that baby all over, getting her saliva into that tiny nick, you now have a hot baby. And if the mother can't bring him enough food, he'll peel out of the nest and look for more." That's a baby we can't take—unless we take him in with the idea of putting him down as humanely as possible.

"We'll have to consider each case very carefully—and I'll make the decisions," I told my staff. "I don't want

Our lovely new sign. (*Photography by Chris Mills.*)

At the fledgling tree . . . here I'm feeding a cedar waxwing.

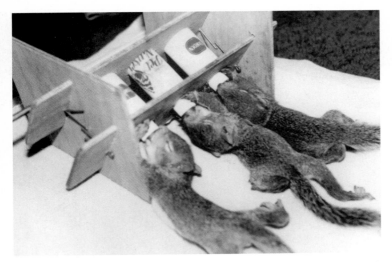

This is a feeding station we devised to accommodate several nursing mammals at one time. It works beautifully. *(Photograph by Beuna Kowacz.)*

A typical scene in my Langhorne kitchen . . . Penelope, my calico cat, is eating her breakfast while a juvenile robin waits to get into her dish.

Canada geese and female roans in one of the wading pools. Most of these birds are recovering patients, free to leave when they're ready. *(Photography by Chris Mills.)*

An adorable and slightly wet skunk.

This pileated woodpecker was found at the base of a telephone pole and we guessed he might have been shocked.
He was able to eat, but couldn't stand on his feet and slowly
deteriorated. He was such a charming bird—it broke our
hearts when he died. *(Photograph by Diane Nickerson.)*

Yetti, my poodle, mothers everything. The fawn knows her,
but wouldn't allow a strange dog to come near.
(Photography by Richard Esher.)

A young kestrel perches on my shoulder.

An opossum. *(Photograph by Ted Cooper.)*

Sammy feeding Precious when she was
still coming in for her bottle.

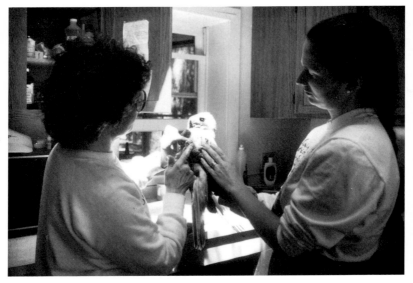

Diane is helping me trim the beak of a red-tailed hawk. In the wild, catching and eating prey would keep its beak trimmed. While it's with us, it needs our assistance.
(Photography by Chris Mills.)

The lovely Sabrina, shortly before she returned to her pond.

anyone else to do that." I also told them I thought we all ought to get rabies shots. "That's up to you," I said.

"It's also up to you to decide whether or not you want to go along with this new policy. How do you feel about it?"

Noreen, Maia, and Diane were my year-round staff. All three of them said yes.

It wasn't long before we had an opportunity to put our new raccoon policy into practice. We took in five baby 'coons from three different nests. They all came from normal, healthy, functioning families that had been disrupted by human activities. We put them in an isolette and then transferred them to boxes. Debbie and Leah were married now, but Sammy was home, and once more we had raccoons underfoot and in our cereal. But not in our beds. We kept the windows closed. And as soon as the 'coons were able to go outside, we took them out in cages and left the doors open. Lately, during the day, they've taken to sleeping under the cage where we keep recuperating broad-winged hawks. They're not the first animals to have found this spot. The cage itself is twelve feet high and five feet wide, with a solid wood floor and wire sides and top, and doweling between the bird and the wire. It's fastened onto the back of the barn and rests on a stone foundation. Some years back, one of the stones came loose, leaving a small cavelike opening, the kind a small animal can really appreciate. We never put the stone back because the foundation is perfectly sturdy without it, and the cave is almost always occupied. It's a fine place for our young raccoons—good and dry, and not accessible to anybody. After dark they come out, run up the trees and play, and wait for us to bring them food. We can't allow them to run up our legs and onto our shoulders, but if no one else is around, and I get a chance to do what I really love, I do it: I reach down and run my hand along a warm, soft, furry body.

What I'd like to be able to do is innoculate the 'coons I treat before I release them. If they're clean, the vaccine will protect them for up to five years—longer than their normal life expectancy. If I can get permission from the state to do this, I would also insist on ear-tagging the innoculated animals. That's the only way we can learn how well the vaccine works for wildlife. It's also the way we can begin to build a barrier against rabies by releasing healthy, protected 'coons.

"If all goes well, we might be able to begin by innoculating these five little ones," I was telling Diane one evening when she came to take charge of the nursery.

I heard a car horn and remembered that Debbie and Leah had come to pick me up. Leah is a beauty consultant and we were going to a cosmetics party. "Omigosh! I forgot they were here!" I said, and ran out the door.

We had decided to go in my Bronco, and the girls were in the back. When I opened the door on the driver's side, there on the seat was a raccoon, sitting back on its heinie, pear-shaped and looking eager to go.

Leah giggled. "He needs some new eyeliner," she said.

For a moment we were back in the days before the threat of rabies. But only for a moment. "C'mon, buddy, out you go," I said and scooted it out of the car.

The 'coon thought I was playing. It darted across the gravel and ran up the fledgling tree. It found company there. The night was young, and there were 'coon things to do.

"Have fun, you guys," I said as we drove away. I meant it. Fun is part of being a raccoon.

4 / What Makes a Rehabber

Rehabbing is chic today. When I was a kid, it wasn't. It was considered strange. On our block, I was the kid who was handy with baby birds and animals, so everybody brought them to me. It's very frustrating for people to come across wildlife in distress, because they usually want to help and they can't. I was willing to care and willing to try, and that was enough. I didn't need any other credentials. All I had to do was hold out my hands, and the animals were mine. The people who brought them went away relieved, and were often surprised when I managed to save them. They hadn't ever heard of anyone working with wild animals. Veterinary medicine was a respected field, but wildlife rehabilitation was—well, strange. There wasn't even a term for it yet.

My parents were embarrassed by what I did, and my passion for doing it. Sometimes, if I heard that neighbors had found an orphaned squirrel or an injured bird, I'd go to see them and talk them out of keeping it. Most people don't know how to care for wild things, so they end up killing them. Or they try to keep them as pets, which also can be disastrous. I never hesitated to tell anyone that I could take better care of the animal. Even at that young age I knew I was able to keep things alive, so I had to have them. I couldn't keep my hands off them. And there was no saying no to me. At one time I had fourteen little songbirds in our house—in my bedroom, in my father's den, and finally in my mother's dining room. I kept them in cages until I could release them.

If one of my friends found a wild animal and wanted to keep it, I tried the same approach. If talk didn't work, I'd bully the kid into giving me the animal. One summer Sunday, when I was wearing my best dress and waiting for a visit from my paternal grandmother, I took on the boy down the street. He was bigger than I was and had a mean streak in him. He and his dog had found a nest of baby bunnies, and he announced that he was going to keep them.

"No, you're not!" I told him.

"Yes, I am!" he said with a sneer as he headed toward his house. He knew very well how I felt about such things. And I knew very well that he was a menace to those bunnies.

I followed him. "You don't know how to feed them!" I shouted, pulling at his shirt to slow him down.

"Who cares? They're mine and I can do what I want with them?"

"You'll hurt them!"

"So what? They're only bunnies."

I grabbed his arm and pulled him off balance just enough for me to snatch the nest of bunnies out of his hands. He wasn't about to let me get away with that and I knew it. I put the bunnies down on the grass and stood in front of them with my fists up and ready. In no time the boy and I were down on the ground, hitting each other as hard as we could, rolling over and over and screaming at each other. I didn't feel a thing. I just knew I was going to win.

At that moment my grandmother, who had the bearing

of a princess, drove down our street. When she saw two dirty little children pounding the sand out of each other right in the middle of the road, she stopped her car and got out.

"Mary Jane!" she said, horrified. "Is that *you*?"

I didn't hear her. I didn't even realize she was there. My nose was bleeding and so was my lip, but I could still punch and that's what I was busy doing.

Leaving her car in the road, my grandmother ran up the block to our house. My mother met her at the door, beautifully dressed and perfectly calm.

"Peg!" my grandmother gasped. "Do you *know* what Mary Jane and . . . ?" That's as far as she got.

My mother smiled as she glanced down the block. "Yes, yes, I know. It'll be all right."

"But she's *fighting*—with that *boy*!"

"I know, I know," my mother said, taking my grandmother by the arm and leading her into the sitting room. "It has something to do with rabbits, I believe. Now, come inside and sit down. You're out of breath."

"Aren't you going to *do* anything about this?" my grandmother said, totally dismayed, yet putting herself completely in my mother's charge.

"There's no need to," my mother assured her. "In due time, Mary Jane will come home—*with* the rabbits and none the worse for wear." She was right. Eventually I won the fight, brought the bunnies home, and lived to fight another day. It seems I've been doing that all my life.

During the early years of my childhood we lived in a section of Philadelphia called Crestmont Farms. Today it's known as Torresdale, and it's a heavily built-up area, but then it was mostly woods and a creek, with plenty of open spaces. Later we moved to Andalusia, in Bucks County, just outside Philadelphia. That was a lot greener than it is today, too. We lived along the river in a beautiful old sixty-three-room mansion on acres of farmland and woods. The house was called Chestnutwood. There were so many trees that at certain times of the year the only way to see our house was from a boat.

My father was a prominent surgeon, and we had the means to live well. I think I might have gone on to become a doctor, too, except that my grades weren't good enough and my father objected. He had had a Victorian upbringing and believed that a woman's only function was to marry and have children. "So you'd better pick a good man," he used to warn me, "because you're used to living high on the hog."

"High on the hog," to me, meant playing in the woods. I loved them. And so did my father. But we loved them in different ways. Early in his life my dad wanted to be a forest ranger, and although he ended up in medicine he never lost his interest in nature or his concern for the ecosystem. He took an opposite route from mine; he was a hunter. He hunted aggressively, anywhere and everywhere, yet he believed that nature had its own laws and that wild things ought to be free. He had an incredible sense of well-being when he was in the woods, and I loved being there with him. In spite of our different points of view, he was a good teacher. He was concerned about the environment even then, and it was through his eyes that I began to see that the earth was in danger.

My mom was the first one to put a bunny in my hands, not as a pet but as a patient. My dad had a hunting dog that used to bring baby rabbits home. He'd find the nests and carry the babies home in his mouth so gently that they didn't have a mark on them. Then he'd plunk them down on our doorstep and sit there whining until my mother came and opened the door. And there he'd be, surrounded by tiny bunnies, and all excited over the gifts he had brought. The babies were too young to look after themselves, and we couldn't put them back because we didn't know where they came from, so my mother always took them in. She couldn't just throw them in the trash, the way some people did. Although it took a lot of her time, she'd raise them until they were old enough to go back to the wild. She was very caring. I was only a couple of years old when she let me help her with them. That's how I learned it was okay to get involved. We'd make up the formulas together, bottle feed the bunnies, and eventually let them go. I can remember my mother showing me how to hold a bunny firmly, without hurting it, while I nursed it with a doll-sized bottle. "It takes time to raise anything," she used to say when a bunny was slow to begin nursing because it didn't know what a bottle was. "It doesn't just happen."

My mother hunted, too, every bit as aggressively as my father, and she's still an excellent shot. But she had more of a feeling for life than my father did. She could take a gun and go out in the fields with my father and kill things. Yet when something helpless was handed to her, her attitude was totally different.

My father's sympathies lay more with the animal's right to be in the world. One day when I was out in the woods with my dog, an Airedale, she chased an opossum up a tree. Airedales can climb trees, so my dog went right up after the 'possum and knocked it down to the ground. It landed at my feet, a bit stunned. It was a large 'possum and I looked it over carefully. There didn't seem to be any wounds or broken bones, so I decided to take it home. I wanted a wild thing of my own.

"No," my father said sternly when I showed him the 'possum. "You have no right to deprive that animal of its freedom."

Of course, I objected, but I didn't get far.

"Here's what you can do," my father said. "You can keep it for two weeks, but I want you to use that time to learn all there is to know about 'possums. At the end of that time, I'm going to ask you some questions, and you'd better have some answers. Then you're going to release the 'possum back into its appropriate habitat— without your dog to help you."

I was disappointed, and at the same time challenged. Even when I was helping my mother with the baby bunnies, I wanted to hold onto them in the beginning, but by the time they were old enough to be released, I was ready to let them go. Sometimes my mother would have to prod me by saying, "No, no, Mary Jane, it's time to give them back"—and then, there were always so many others that needed care. I feel the same way today, and I've learned to give things up much more quickly. It doesn't seem right to hold onto them.

By the end of two weeks, I was an expert on 'possums. I read everything I could find in the library, but I learned even more just by being with the animal and watching it for hours every day. I saw that wild animals weren't like my dog and cat. They can't adapt well to civilization, and they don't benefit from it. They're primitives, and they need to be in their natural environment in order to function well. Where was an opossum going to use that marvelous, gripping, ropelike tail if I kept it in a cage? And what would happen to the part of its psyche that depended on the skill of that tail to help it maneuver high up in the trees when predators were around? By the time my father was ready to test my knowledge of 'possums, I was on his side. I knew they had to be free.

From that time on, I was more than my mother's helper. When Dad's dog brought home a nest of bunnies, Mom would put a few of them in my hands and say, "Here, you take care of these."

My father fed our family off the land. He was far ahead of his time in realizing that most of the food we buy in the stores is contaminated with harmful chemicals and additives, and the only way for him to provide us with safe food was to raise it—or shoot it—himself. He farmed organically, and he did all the work himself. We had beautiful formal gardens on our land, and in between the carefully trimmed shrubs, Daddy planted vegetables. He also looked after our livestock and fed them on organically grown feed. Everything our family ate came from our land—our vegetables, fruit, milk, butter and eggs, and our meat. Even our fish came from the river that bordered our land.

For a while I followed the family tradition and bred rabbits for food. I was allowed to keep the money I made from selling the meat, but I couldn't bring myself to kill the rabbits. My father did that, and he would let me know when it was going to happen so I wouldn't be around for the slaughter. Usually he'd do it on a weekend while I was staying with a girlfriend. But I dreaded coming home to the empty cages and knowing what had happened to the rabbits, so after a little while I decided to go out of business. I couldn't deliberately raise something to be killed.

It seemed that my father's attitude toward killing something and my passion for saving it were always in conflict. And sometimes my father seemed to go out of his way to bedevil me. One day we were out driving, my mother and father up front and my grandmother and I in back, and we saw a pigeon in the road up ahead. It was a lovely white one, and I leaned forward to get a better look. Suddenly the car shot forward as my father pressed his foot down on the accelerator. I thought he hadn't seen the pigeon, and I shouted, "Look out! There's a pigeon!" In the same instant I realized that my father had already seen the bird and knew exactly what he was doing. He wanted to kill it.

"Don't! Don't! Don't!" I screamed at him. I pounded at his shoulders with my fists while my grandmother tried to pull me back. "No, no, no! Sh-h-h! Sh-h-h!" she kept saying in a hoarse whisper, close to my ear. "No, Mary Jane, don't do that! You know how your father is."

The pigeon couldn't get off the ground fast enough. As our car ran over it, I shrieked for its agony and struggled to get out of my grandmother's arms.

My father's eyes met mine in the rearview mirror. He was smiling. "Now what are you going to do?" he teased me.

The thought of that dead bird back there in the road and the frustration of being helpless to do anything about it, made me reckless. I didn't care what my father did to me. I pulled free of my grandmother and leaned forward, screaming at the back of my father's head, "I don't have to *do*, 'cause when you meet your Maker, you're going to have to account for this! You murdered that pigeon! You did it on purpose!"

My mother shushed me and reached for my striking hands. I saw the flash of anger in my father's eyes as my grandmother grabbed me around the waist and pulled me back onto the seat. "Hush, child, hush!" she whispered as she put her hand over my mouth to keep me quiet. "Don't confront your father."

Later, my grandmother tried to comfort me by saying, "Mary Jane, the world is full of pigeons. You mustn't take this so seriously."

I shook my head. "The world is full of people, too, Grandma," I said. "But it's not okay to run over them with a car."

"Well, people would protest if that happened. But pigeons are different, darling," my grandmother said.

"No, not to me," I said. "Somebody has to scream for them, too."

That night, when I was in bed, I kept thinking of my father. He laughed at what he had done, and he thought I was a screwball to get upset about it. But it wasn't going to be so funny when he had to account for all his killing, because it *wasn't* okay. I loved my father, but I worried about him.

All of us kill in one way or another in order to survive. In order to stop killing, we'd have to stop eating, because everything is part of the food chain. Yet, to kill something deliberately—and for no practical, life-sustaining reason—that's different.

I don't understand this desire to kill, yet I come across it often. I don't use my fists to fight it now. When I was a child, I couldn't see beyond my rage and my need to stop the killing. But now I weep for those who feel they need to do it. Whatever causes it—their karma or an underdeveloped sensitivity to living things—they're missing an important, wonderful part of life. And I believe they *will* be judged.

I mourn for the person who does the killing even more than the creature killed, because I believe that a life ended is a life begun. I believe that when a life is ended, that being—whether feathered, furred, or flesh and blood—is lifted onto another plane of existence. It goes on to a better life, and I'm happy for it. But I mourn for the person who ended that creature's life to satisfy his own pleasure. He wasn't trying to send that animal's soul into another dimension; he was acting out of a primitive impulse to destroy. Someday he'll have to answer for that, and his answer may not be adequate. Instead of going on, he may have to go back and make up for his mistakes.

I'm sure it was my mother's gentleness with helpless young animals that got me started as a rehabber. But I was also motivated by my father's opposition. From the time my mother put a baby bunny in my hands, I knew I would always take care of animals. And the more my father opposed me, the more determined I was to get around the obstacles he put in my way. At one point I wanted to become a veterinarian so I could apply some medical training to the care of wild things, but when my father refused to pay for my education, I decided to educate myself in whatever ways I could. My father would never share his medical knowledge with me, so I tried one remedy or method and then another, hoping that something would work. Now, however, he often comes to my rescue with medical techniques and advice.

Many nights I went to bed thinking about an animal I was trying to save, and the answer to my problem often came to me in my sleep. It always seemed so logical. When I woke up, I'd think, "Maybe it won't work." But it always came down to this: the animal was going to die if I didn't do something, so if I killed it trying something, then the animal and I were no better or worse off than we were before I tried to save it. But if I learned how to save it, then we both were a lot better off. I had nothing to lose. So I'd do what seemed logical for me to do, and most times I was successful. When I wasn't, I could usually figure out what I'd done wrong and do it right the next time.

Today rehabbers don't have to learn so much by trial and error. While there isn't one specific course leading to a degree in wildlife rehabilitation, there are several intensive seminars available, which can save a lot of guesswork. And the requirements for a permit are increasingly demanding. You have to take exams, and after you get your permit, you have to keep up with new procedures by taking a seminar at least once every two years. If you don't, your license won't be renewed—and it comes up for renewal every year. Thanks to these requirements, I'm seeing better-prepared, better-educated people coming into the field.

But when it comes to making a living wage as a rehabber, you're still on your own. That's another area where my father's opposition helped me. First of all, he told me I couldn't do what I wanted to do because he wouldn't help me. So I did it without his help. It was almost as if, by closing a door, he forced me to become strong enough to push the door open. Then, when everybody told me I was crazy to work with wild animals because I couldn't make a living doing it, I didn't pay much attention, because I had already come up against bigger obstacles. I got other jobs to bring in money while I worked with wild things. I cleaned houses, I sewed, I was a salesclerk in a men's clothing store—I did the kind of work that allowed me to set my own hours so I could be with my children and my animals when they needed me.

Most rehabbers have to do the same thing. My salaried part-time staff members can't support themselves on what they earn working with me. So we're always on the lookout for flexible part-time jobs they can do on the side, especially during the winter months when The Aark is relatively quiet. I'm amazed at the material sacrifices these women—and some men—are willing to make in order to do the kind of work where they feel they can make even a small difference in their world. Apparently, I'm not the only screwball on the planet.

Eventually even my father began to change his mind about my work, although it took a long time. Two things helped: I moved away from home, and the environment became an important issue all over the world. Once I was out on my own, among strangers who had no pre-conceived notions of what I ought to be, I increasingly felt accepted for what I was. I think that's true of us all. The people we grow up with may overlook our talents, and then, when someone else points them out, they're surprised. All of a sudden, something previously consid-ered unconventional or silly takes on value because someone else appreciates it. I had been concerned about the environment since I was a child, and that was some-thing my father could share with me. But he thought I was a fool to commit so much of my time to convincing people that the earth needed their help. He wasn't alone in that; for years while I was growing up, people would roll their eyes and look at the heavens when I got on my soapbox.

Then things began to change. What my father and I had seen much earlier has finally become so evident it can't be ignored. Crystal-clear lakes have become foul-smelling mudholes, the air we breathe has begun to choke us, trees that have been healthy for generations are beginning to die in spite of everything we do to save them, birds and animals that feed on plants contami-nated by chemicals have begun giving birth to deformed babies, some species are dying out before their evolution-ary time is up. Human life itself has been threatened.

I've gone from being "Crazy Jane" and "The Witch" to "Saint Jane" as more people have begun to hear what

I'm saying about the environment—because they are ready to listen. My job as an assistant naturalist at the Churchville Nature Center was the first time I got paid for teaching people about the ecosystem, yet I had been doing it all my life. Suddenly, I wasn't "peculiar" anymore; I was an "expert."

My work began to attract a lot of media attention. Newspapers did feature stories about me, and local television stations invited me to be on their shows. I didn't mention any of that to my father because by that time I had given up trying to prove to him that I was doing serious work. My mother knew about it, but she still treated me like a little girl who might someday come to her senses and make something of her life.

Eventually, though, my father began to hear about me from his friends. "Say, did you see that article about Mary Jane?" someone would say to him. "She's doing some really important work!" A doctor he knew came up and slapped him on the back with a "Hey, George, isn't that your daughter who's working with those animals? I saw her on TV last night and, I tell ya, she really spelled out what's happening on this earth of ours. Good God, you must be proud of her—look at what's she's done against all those odds!"

"Oh, sure," my dad said, trying not to reveal that he didn't know what the man was talking about. "Yeah—yeah, that's my kid."

Then my father went to a party where he was introduced to some of the guests as "Mary Jane's father." That did it. When he told me about it, he said, "You know, it used to be that you were my daughter. Now I'm your father." And he laughed affectionately. Maybe he still didn't understand exactly what I was doing, but obviously he thought it was okay.

When I first went into rehabbing, it was primarily a man's world. It wasn't that women couldn't do the work;

we just didn't have the training men had. And without an adequate education, we didn't have the power to make things happen. We didn't know how to fight our way into a man's world and demand access to the information men had had all their lives. We were good at nurturing, but we didn't know beans about management. We wanted to work with animals, period. We didn't realize that you can't do anything without an organization to support your efforts. Men know that because they have been doing it for centuries, but it wasn't part of our history. All we could do was be sympathetic to each other when we were perceived as cute little bunny-huggers who meant well but really didn't know anything.

Not all men saw us that way, however. I had to fight very hard to be taken seriously, but I had help from a few men who were able to see beyond the bunny-hugger stereotype to what I was doing. In fact, it was their respect that made me take myself more seriously. I began to realize that I could make sound decisions about matters of life and death—and I could carry them out.

One of those men was Tom Fitzpatrick. He was my daughter Leah's pediatrician, and all my children love him. Now he's the pediatrician for my granddaughters. He wears jeans to work and gets right down on the floor with his patients. He's concerned about the ecosystem, and an ardent birder; if he sees a hawk in the sky, he'll run out of his office to get a better look at it. He and his wife became part of our family. They also became part of my work. Tom loves babies, all kinds of babies, and he's even helped me bottlefeed baby animals.

He was the first professional person who believed in what I was doing—and this, mind you, was twenty-five years ago, when I kept my patients in my kitchen, in cages all over the floor, on the countertops and the kitchen table. I had only a few birds and animals then, but each one was a challenge because there was so little medical information available to me. I wasn't trying to intrude on the territory of veterinarians or medical doctors; I didn't want to do anything I wasn't supposed to do without a license. I just wanted some advice.

For instance, I once treated a baby squirrel with an infected knee. It would die if I couldn't bring down the inflammation, but I wasn't sure how much medicine I should use because the squirrel was so tiny. Finally I asked Tom, "What would you do for a preemie baby like this?"

He thought about it for a moment. Then he said, "What have you been using?"

"Hot compresses."

"Why not an antibiotic?"

"I don't know how much to use—this baby's so small."

"Let me think about it," he said. "Meantime, stay with the compresses."

He began scribbling on a piece of paper. Starting with the amount of antibiotics suitable for a premature infant, he kept reducing the dosage in proportion to the squirrel's weight. "This ought to do it," he said, handing me the paper. I used the dosage he suggested, and the squirrel recovered. Its leg was fine.

In days gone by, doctors used to drive out to a farm, deliver a couple's baby, and then go out to the barn to treat their sick cow. Today, that's not legal; medical licenses are very specific as to what a doctor can and cannot do. Tom was always careful to observe those limitations. He never practiced medicine on my animals, and he never gave me the means to attempt to practice it. But he shared his concern for all living things with me and my children—and, most important, he helped me recognize what I was treating. Back in those days, rehabbers' methods were so primitive that it makes me weep to remember them. So many lives were lost that could have been saved if only someone with information had simply taken the trouble to listen to our questions and give us straightforward answers. It's not surprising that I'm grateful to Tom: at a crucial time in my career, when

I was getting to the point where I began to think, "Maybe everybody else is right . . . maybe this can't be done," he was willing to help me grope my way toward more sophisticated methods of treating wild animals.

I'd tell him about an animal that wasn't responding to my usual care, and he'd say, "Maybe it's dehydrated." Then he'd suggest ways to introduce fluids into the animal's body when the animal was too weak to take fluids on its own. From there I went on to learn that there was a whole body of information known as fluid therapy, which has since saved thousands of my patients.

Once, when I brought Leah in for a checkup, I saw some of Tom's instruments laid out on a table. There aren't any instruments especially designed for rehabbers, and I was always on the lookout for tools I could adapt to my needs, so I looked over the assortment. "Gee, Tom, I could use something like this," I said, picking up an instrument I had often seen in my father's office when I was a child. It was a hemostat. Hemostats look like eyebrow tweezers, but longer, and the ends are rounded instead of pointed. "Where can I get one?"

"It's for clamping the skin together when you're suturing a wound," he said, and then he remembered I was a surgeon's daughter. "Got something else in mind?"

I often used instruments designed for something entirely different from my needs, but as long as they worked well, I didn't care. I held up a hemostat, smiling at the thought of what I could accomplish with it. "Maggots," I said.

"Ugh-h-h!" Tom groaned.

"No—beautiful! I've been using eyebrow tweezers, but they're too sharp and too short. Maggots go down so deep that they're hard to get to. With this, I could go into a hole and pull the little bastards right out."

Tom was shaking his head, but smiling.

"Where can I get one?" I asked him.

"Any medical supply store," he said.

*　　*　　*

People like Tom understood my hunger to learn. He knew that, to a rehabber, even the simplest tool or the smallest scrap of scientific information was like a miracle.

I don't kid myself about the animals I save. What I do for them allows them to go right back into the food chain, which is where they would be if I hadn't touched them. But that's the way the food chain is, and it's not my place to change it. Nature may be beautiful at times, but it's very unforgiving and very tough. I put animals back into a much crueler world, but I try to put them back in good condition. I always hope that what I do for them enables them to live a normal number of years and reproduce their kind, which is what they are meant to do. They could do it on their own, if man didn't interfere. So my job, as I see it, is to undo a little bit of the damage man does. I try to *uninterfere.*

Here at The Aark we serve the animals, but in order to serve them better we have to educate human beings to their needs. It would be absurd for me to think I make an appreciable difference in the animal population of this planet. Of course, I don't! The twenty-five hundred birds and animals I see each year are nothing compared to the whole ecosystem; I'd have to see millions to change things. But through the animals I see I can reach people, and that's where I can make an impact. It took me a long time to realize that this is the area where rehabbing makes a difference. It's like throwing a stone in a pond and seeing ripples reach out farther and farther until an enormous amount of water is moving. When one family brings one bird or one squirrel into The Aark, we confirm immediately that it's okay to care. We explain what might have happened to the animal, what should have been done, what can be done, what they can do, and what we can do. When that family leaves, they have a different way of looking at the earth. They see that it isn't there for us to conquer, and that if we don't learn how to co-exist with other forms of life, soon there won't be any life at all. And people pass this message on.

Things are beginning to change. I hope it's not too late. More people are paying attention to the earth's needs. They're telling their political representatives that they'd better pay attention, too. Now we need to bring the message to our children so they can grow up with it. I'd like to see more schools teach planet co-existence to their students: humans with humans, humans with animals, humans with vegetation, stones, water, air.

Co-existing with our environment isn't easy. Sometimes our heart tells us one thing and our head another, so we have to decide between them. It's taken me a long time to be able to do that, and I still struggle with it.

Banding birds, for instance, is something I don't like to do, although I recognize the value of it. Scientifically, I'm in favor of it. Morally and emotionally, I'm not. When birds are trapped and banded and then released, we get some accurate information about their ages and their flight. This is especially important when a species is endangered. It helps us to know that a broad-winged hawk, banded and released in Pennsylvania, eventually shows up in Argentina. But the number of banded birds that are re-trapped is very small, and many of them go on to die where no one finds them.

I stopped banding great-horned owls because I saw too many of them tearing the bands off their legs. Obviously the bands were uncomfortable, and an owl has a hard enough time surviving in our world. Besides, the ones we treat are already at a disadvantage, so why make survival more difficult for them by putting a band on their leg? I don't band crows anymore, either. In winter people bring them to us when they find them stranded on the ground with iced bands. Crows are ground-feeders, so they're more likely to walk around in snow, and when a band gets iced, it's hard for the bird to fly. Since crows aren't rare or endangered, I don't band them.

I don't band many birds at all anymore, not since someone said to me, "Do you have the right to put your mark on a bird forever?"

"I never thought about it that way," I said. When I did think about it, I came to the conclusion that I didn't have the right—unless a species is endangered and any information we can get may help to save it from extinction.

I can argue either side of the issue, depending on which part of me is doing the arguing, my head or my heart. It's the same with hunting.

Whenever I hear a gun go off, the shot goes through my heart. I've always been that way, and I don't think I'll ever change. But that's my emotional response to hunting. My intellect sees it in a different way. It tells me there is a need for the responsible hunter in today's world.

Man has eliminated so many natural predators that now he's the only one left. There is very little habitat available for animals, and in some areas where hunting is prohibited, the animal population is becoming so dense that there isn't enough food to go around. Like it or not—and I don't—there is a need for culling. We have to do what nature used to do before we interfered: protect and preserve enough animals to reproduce healthy new generations. That's what I call responsible hunting. But nature's way of culling is more effective than ours. When natural predators do the killing, they eliminate the oldest and the weakest of the species because they're the easiest to catch. When man goes out with a gun or a bow and arrow, he looks for the biggest and best of the species. He gets trophies for eliminating the healthiest, most beautiful animals—which means that more of the weaker ones are left to reproduce. That's not responsible culling. If I had my way I'd give the prizes for the worst specimens, because the only way a hunter can truly render a service to the ecosystem is to follow nature's example: pick off the animals that have passed their robust years, or those that will never have them.

Most people who aren't hunters have some misconceptions about those who are. For instance, it isn't true that a hunter hits something every time he takes a shot. Far from it. If you have ever sat in a deer stand waiting for deer to come through, or walked the fields hunting pheasant, you know that a hunter doesn't get many chances to shoot, and he misses more than he hits. He's like the hawk, which misses its prey about 90 percent of the time. Unfortunately it's the irresponsible hunters who get the publicity. What we hear about is the jackass who shot the farmer's cow, or the one who went over his limit and beat up the conservation officer who tried to stop him. They don't outnumber the good hunters, but they do make bad news, and bad news sells. We don't hear as much about the hunters who obey our game laws strictly and teach conservation to young people. Most of us aren't acquainted with the hunter who simply loves being close to the earth, or the one who takes a gun along with him during the hunting season but never fires a shot.

At The Aark, most of our animals are brought in by small children. The reasons are obvious: children are closer to the earth, and they're not preoccupied with all the concerns that preoccupy adults. When they see a bird or an animal in trouble, they rush in, unafraid, without a lot of preconceived notions about bugs and dirt. They're not worried about whether they're doing the right thing. It's a matter of something small and young relating to something small and young. Usually these children come in accompanied by their parents, and sometimes it's obvious that the parents really would rather not get involved. They want to support the child in getting help for the animal, but they're holding the animal out at arm's length. Not the children. They're not afraid to touch and care and get messed up.

After children, surprisingly, the largest group is hunters; they bring us a lot of patients. Most hunters are people who love being in the woods at any time of the year. Because they're familiar with the behavior of animals in their normal habitat, they're quick to notice something that isn't right. They're also able to make a better judgment about whether the animal needs help. People who scream, "I love animals!" or "Poor darling, it knows I'm helping it," will often rush in and snatch something that doesn't need to be rescued. They'll take baby birds out of a nest because the mother isn't in the nest with them, and they don't know enough to look for her nearby. But a hunter knows better. He'll wait and watch, because he knows the mother bird has to go and get food for the babies. If he sees her come back to the nest, he'll leave the babies alone. He knows they're okay.

Sometimes, when a hunter brings me an animal, he's a little shy about identifying himself. He probably assumes he's going to get a lecture. He'll say something like, "I have to tell you that I'm a hunter—and I guess you don't like that."

I'm very quick to say, "That's okay. As long as you're a responsible hunter, there's a place for you. I'm not going to discuss hunting because I'm not here to take sides. I'm here to help this creature you've brought me." I tell the same thing to my volunteers and staff, because many of them are emotionally opposed to hunting, just as I am. But we can't allow that to interfere with our work. "We're not here to preach," I tell them. "I don't want to drive away the hunter or the activist, so if I catch any of you preaching, I'll ask you to leave, because you're not serving the animals by doing that."

Sometimes a hunter will bring in an animal that's been shot by somebody else, and he hopes I can fix it up. Usually this is a man who is out in the woods carrying a gun, intending to shoot something, yet when he comes across a wounded animal he picks it up and brings it to The Aark. He's angry because someone shot the animal but didn't finish the job. I don't have to ask him why he didn't finish the job himself; he volunteers the information: "Well, it was on the ground, and it wasn't my shot. I just couldn't shoot it, because it isn't right. That's not what hunting is about." I hear this often, and to me it means the hunter is on the brink of not shooting a gun anymore.

Occasionally a hunter will bring me an animal he's wounded, and he'll say, "I'll never, ever, do this again! I can't stand it. I didn't realize. . . ." Usually this is a person who hasn't been a hunter for long. It's a shame when people have to go to this extreme, but sometimes they have to witness an animal's suffering before they discover they don't need to kill. I do my best to support them and relieve their discomfort. I don't want hunters— either those new at the game or oldtimers—to leave a wounded animal because they just can't put up with the hard time they get when they go for help. I want them to go home feeling good about themselves because they took the time to help an animal—and maybe the next time they go in the woods to get a shot, instead of pulling the trigger, they just won't.

I have great admiration too, for conservation officers— or, as we used to call them, game wardens. With very few exceptions, they are people who care. Why else would they take such a difficult job that doesn't pay well and draws flak from everybody, environmentalists as well as hunters? Most people think their taxes pay the salaries of conservation officers. Well, they don't. Their salaries are paid by hunting license fees, so they don't owe the taxpayer anything. If they help the taxpayer, it's a favor. And a lot of them do a lot of favors. They don't have to bring us sick or orphaned animals. But they do it often. They don't have to drive long distances on their own time to get help for wildlife. But they do. Often.

The first time I saw Bill Wasserman, a Montgomery County conservation officer, I said to myself, "Here comes trouble!" Bill's a big guy, nice looking, young, with a strong muscular body, a real macho type if you go by first impressions, and I did. He was also wearing a badge—but not a hat. His hat was in his hands, and in his hat was a litter of bunnies. He had come to my dining room door, and when I opened it I saw a big hulk with a gun, handcuffs, a uniform, and a hat full of bunnies and bunny shit.

"Ma'am," he said, "I found these baby rabbits." He seemed embarrassed and spoke fast. "The mother got killed on the road, as far as I can tell. Now I know you must get a lot of rabbits, and God knows they aren't scarce, so we don't need more. But, ma'am, could you take them in? Please?"

"Omigosh! Sure! Come in," I told him. He ducked his head coming in. I took his hat and headed for my kitchen, which served as my nursery in those days. "Let me get some milk in them—and then let me give you a cup of coffee." I knew he had driven a long distance to get to us.

When he looked around at all the cages and some of the animals running loose in my kitchen, he said, "Do you do this all by yourself?"

"Right now, yes." In those days I didn't have volunteers.

"I feel real bad, putting another burden on you," he said. "Seems like you've got enough to feed right now."

"No, really, I'm glad you brought them," I said. "I would have done the same thing."

"I couldn't just leave them to die, ma'am," he said.

I gave him back his hat. It was a mess. "I know," I said. "I understand."

Bill has been back several times. And he's not the only conservation officer who knows the way to The Aark.

Construction workers bring us patients, too. They're usually upset when they come in, because they've been clearing land with monster-sized equipment and all of a sudden have discovered a tiny animal in their path. I hate to see land developed, but I'm sympathetic to the guy on the bulldozer. He can't see when he's coming into a nest. He may or may not care what happens to the animals in it, but it's not his decision to rape the land. He's at the end of the chain of events, and he's struggling to make a living. The rapist is the man in the expensive silk suit who sits in an office and cuts the deal.

When it comes to appearances, I'm like most people: I try not to pigeonhole them, but I end up doing it anyway. I make snap judgments and usually I'm wrong. When I see big, rough-looking men tearing up the earth, I assume they must be insensitive. Then, all of a sudden, one of them will show up at my door—hot, sweaty, and in a big hurry to get back to his bulldozer. "Hey, lady," he'll say, "can you do something with this stuff?" And I see a baby squirrel peeking out of his shirt, and of course the squirrel has peed all over him. "I just can't let—I made those guys stop," the man will say, pointing in the direction where I know a development is going up. He doesn't give me time to respond. "I'll probably get in trouble for this, but—here!" he says. And with that, he puts the squirrel in my hands and runs off. I'm always caught offguard by the softness of these tough guys. On the other hand, I'm often horrified to discover that people who appear to be kind, caring, and non-threatening will walk right past a baby bunny in trouble because they think, "I can't get involved—I might get sued or something." They'll chase squirrels away because they eat birdseed, and they'll saturate their shrubs with chemicals that kill far more than bugs. I'm still learning that you can't judge people by the way they look.

But sometimes people can change. Once they understand what they're doing wrong, and how much harm they're doing to the earth, most people are on our side. The fact that I get calls all year round from men and women who want to be volunteers proves it.

Of course, I also get my share of angry callers, or callers who become angry after they discover that I can't do what they want me to do. A few days ago a woman called to get help for a raccoon that had been hit by a car outside her house. We were very busy that day, and no one was available to go and get the animal.

"Can you bring it in?" I asked the caller.

"No, I can't. My husband has the car today." She couldn't think of anyone who could drive the animal to us.

"Then I can't help you," I told her, and suggested that she call her conservation officer. I went on to explain that even if the animal could be brought in, I'd probably have to put it down.

"Why?" she demanded. "I thought you could save animals."

"I'd have to see it first, but in the case of raccoons, I can't offer you much hope. It's the rabies situation—we can't take the chance if we don't know where the 'coon comes from." I tried to explain why we had to be careful, but she wasn't listening.

She was furious. "I can't believe what I'm hearing!" she said. "I heard you were an animal lover, but you're not! You're cruel! I think you're stupid, too!" Then she hung up.

We don't get many calls like that, but they always leave me stunned. Sometimes I feel physically ill for a day or two, because my spirituality has been attacked. Usually it happens when people don't like what I have to say about what should be done with an animal. Very often I tell people to let the animal go, but they want to keep it as a pet. Eventually they get bitten and then they call again because they want to get rid of the animal. That's when I tell them what they did wrong and try to explain how they can do things better the next time. Believe me, that's not welcome advice.

I believe there's a lesson in everything, so when a caller gets angry enough to become abusive I go back over our conversation, looking for ways I might have handled things better. "Maybe I was a little short," I tell myself. "Maybe I could have used a softer tone of voice.

Maybe I didn't say what needed to be said. How can I say it better?" Sometimes I'll stop short in the middle of a conversation and say, "Hey, wait a minute—let's both stop. How about, I'll apologize to you, because I must have offended you, even though I didn't mean to. Let's start again and take it from the animal's point of view." And sometimes that works.

When I get discouraged, I look forward to the 3:00 A.M. feeding in the nursery because everything is very quiet then, and there's no one except me and the animals. It's like being "Crazy Jane" again, knowing I can keep things alive if they really want to live. I always offer a prayer of thanks for the little ones that were born that day and for those that came in to us. I don't necessarily talk to God—that is, G-o-d, with a capital G. God is an easy word to use because most people understand what you mean by it, even though it means different things to different people. To me it means a supreme energy force that is present in all of life and all living things. In a very small way, I'm a part of it. So is everyone and everything that lives. I'm a part of the animals, and they're a part of me. I can feel their pain, and they can feel my comfort. Sometimes, when an animal feels well enough, it'll turn around and bite me, but that's okay. It's the animal's way of telling me it doesn't need me anymore and wants to be free. We human beings tend to nurse things longer than necessary, and the animal, in its infinite wisdom, will bite me as if to say, "Enough, enough." But sometimes an animal doesn't want to be saved. I believe that we all have a choice about whether to live or die, and we make our choices subconsciously. If an animal has made its choice, I can't change it, and the animal will die.

But if it chooses to try again, that's where I come into the picture. I try to give it that chance. That's all a rehabber can do.

5 / House Calls

Ordinarily I don't make house calls. But life at The Aark is rarely ordinary. I make house calls when the bird or animal could become dangerous and people might get hurt trying to rescue it because they don't know what to do. Or when the situation is so unusual that I have to be there to see the lay of the land before I can come up with a rescue plan. I don't make house calls when I'm overwhelmed with patients. I won't leave animals I'm already working with to go after one I may not be able to catch or one that might be dead by the time I get to it. So, no, I don't make house calls unless I can spare the time and there's a chance I can really help.

On one especially cold January night several years ago, a call came in from a man who said, "We've got this emergency! Our swan, Sabrina—"

"Your what?" I said. "Who?"

It seems the man and his wife, who lived on a farm near New Hope, Pennsylvania, had been adopted by a swan that flew in several months earlier and took up residence on their pond. The couple were delighted that she wanted to stay, and she was rather friendly, which is unusual for a swan, so they put out all sorts of food for her. And they called her Sabrina.

"She's frozen into the pond," the man told me. "We could see she wasn't feeling well the past couple of days, but we couldn't get her to come in."

"How did she behave?" I asked him.

"She was off her feed—and her eyes weren't right."

"Not right, how?"

"Kind of runny."

"That may be why she got frozen in," I said. "Usually a bird will get out of water that's freezing over. But not if it's sick."

"Her whole body's frozen in!" the man said. He was trying hard to stay calm, but it wasn't easy. "How can we get her out?"

I started to tell him that he or his wife would have to crawl out on the ice to get the swan.

"I'll do that," he said.

"Then tie a rope around yourself and let your wife hold onto the other end. You could go through, and if that happens, you'll need someone there to pull you out."

I began to think about the two of them, in the dark, in the cold, going out on the ice, and I didn't like the idea at all. They would have to bring some hot water out with them to melt the ice around the swan's body. It would be tricky.

"This is getting too complicated," I said. "Tell me how to get to your place." He gave me directions, and I took Billy, one of our volunteers, with me. I had every intention of going out on the ice myself.

"Why would you want to do that?" Billy asked.

"Because I probably weigh less than the man who called," I told him, "and I know what to do."

Billy knew me too well. "Are those your only reasons?" he said.

"Smartass," I said. "You know I like adventure. Help me load this rope in the car."

I rarely have a swan at The Aark. It's quite common to find them in Delaware and Maryland, in the Chesapeake Bay area, but not in Pennsylvania. Sometimes people with ponds on their property buy a pair of swans because they're such aggressive, territorial birds that they keep out other waterfowl. With swans standing guard, the only other birds that get in are Canada geese, which swans seem to like. It's not that swans don't like other birds, but if too many of them take over a small body of water, it can be dangerous for them. There won't be enough food to go around, and too much fecal matter gets in the water. Eventually botulism sets in and the birds come down with all sorts of problems. A body of water solid with waterfowl may be picturesque, but it isn't healthy.

New Hope is only a few miles away, and the directions were good, so it didn't take us long to find the farm. The man and woman had already rescued the swan. They had tied each end of a long rope around their waists so they were fastened to each other in case one of them went through the ice. They put some buckets of hot water in a small, light rowboat and pushed the boat ahead of them on the ice as they crawled out toward the bird. Then they poured the hot water around the swan to make the ice let go of her feathers. As the ice gave way, they pulled the swan free and climbed into the boat for safety.

Billy and I followed the couple into their barn where they were trying to keep the swan warm. She was under some blankets, and all the lights were on.

I knelt down to look at the bird. She was very large, but she didn't fight me. She was too weak. "Turn off some of the lights," I said. "The blankets are enough for now." Birds are no different from people when they're suffering from hypothermia: if you bring their body temperature up too fast, they'll die. Moving the swan from the ice to the barn made for a big change in temperature, and I wanted her to settle into it for a while before we applied any more heat.

I felt her feet. The body temperature of a swan changes according to whatever surrounds its feet, and hers were ice cold. Even in winter, as long as a swan's feet are in open water the bird won't freeze because its feet can keep moving and acting like a thermostat for the rest of its body. When the water starts icing over, the swan gets out, but Sabrina hadn't been able to do that because she was sick. When swans are on land, they pull their feet under them to protect the soft flesh from the cold. Their other sensitive areas are their eyes and beaks, and they protect them by tucking their faces under their wings. Their feathers act as insulation to keep their body temperature at 103 degrees. Sabrina's was far below that.

The couple were standing near me. In the dim light, I couldn't exactly see them, but I knew they were there. "How is she?" the man said.

"I'm not sure she can make it," I told him. "It's too early to tell."

Finally I felt a slight change in Sabrina's feet. They were a little bit warmer to the touch. "I'd like to take her back with me," I said. "Her temperature's starting to come up, and that's a good sign, but I can do much more for her at The Aark." With the couple's permission, Billy and I lifted the listless white bird onto the backseat of my car and I climbed in beside her. Handling a large bird takes practice, but I can do it in my sleep. I grab the bird with one hand and pull it close to me, tucking its wings close to its body, because if one of those wings hits you, it can break an arm or leg. With my other hand, I grasp the bird under its jawbone so I can control its head, because the striking power of that long neck is awesome. But in Sabrina's case, there wasn't any resistance.

The bathtubs at The Aark serve many purposes, and we often have guests in them. We put Sabrina in the downstairs bathtub and filled it with lukewarm water. She needed nourishment, especially fluids, but she wouldn't eat, so I got out my trusty old-fashioned douche bag and put the long, flexible tube down her throat. It was the gentlest way to force-feed her. Once we began feeding her Nutrical and a mash we use for waterfowl, we could see some improvement in her. As her body temperature continued to rise, we gradually increased the heat of the water.

"I think she's going to be all right," I said. Billy agreed.

Sabrina seemed comfortable, even though the bathtub was small for a bird her size. And she certainly was beautiful.

"We can leave her for a while now," I said. It was almost time for the 7:00 A.M. feeding, and I wanted Billy to go home and get some sleep because he had to go to work in a few hours.

Sabrina proved to be the most gracious guest I have ever had in my home. She thanked us by the way she received us. She stayed for ten days, and during that time she and I became good friends. Even though the girls and I knew she was there, it was always startling to open the bathroom door and see a big white bird floating in the tub. Occasionally we'd find her sitting on the toilet. She was eating well on her own and getting her strength back.

Usually, when we have a bird in the downstairs bathroom, we try not to disturb it, so if we have to use a bathroom we go upstairs. But one day I was in a hurry, so I decided to make an exception. Sabrina wasn't the least bit bothered. In fact, she seemed pleased to see me and apparently was ready for a little fun. She began pecking at my legs, and then she started to make swan sounds. I had had so few opportunities to hear a swan that I was fascinated by the range of voices that came out of her, and I stayed there for a long time just listening to her.

There was a knock on the door. "Mom—you okay?" It was Debbie. She must have wondered what happened to me because when it comes to bathrooms, I'm in and out.

"I'm fine," I said. "Sabrina and I are having a conversation, that's all."

"What's she saying?"

That was a good question. I had no idea what Sabrina meant by all those sounds, but I got the feeling that she was enjoying my company. And I certainly enjoyed hers. In fact, during the next few days I spent a lot of my time in the downstairs bathroom, listening to swan sounds and trying to imitate them. That excited Sabrina. I have no idea what I was saying to her, but evidently it was something she liked. She even let me rub her head, which is unusually friendly for a swan. Being able to see a swan and having one in my house was a blessing in itself, but having one talk to me and permit me to touch her was truly an honor.

The severe cold spell broke eventually, and it was time to prepare Sabrina to go back to her pond. She was walking around and opening her huge wings. Her wingspan was much wider than my arms held wide open, and she definitely was outgrowing the bathroom. Her "family" was eager to have her back, but first we had to give her a chance to adjust to the outdoors again. We have a large screened porch on the side of our house, and in the winter I cover it on all three sides with heavy plastic that keeps out the wind but lets the sun in. It's really quite pleasant out there, even warm at times. We moved all the furniture down to one end and put a big tub of water in the middle of the floor so Sabrina could get in and out of it and just have the whole porch to herself. Well, almost to herself. Coincidentally someone had brought in another swan. There was nothing apparently wrong with the bird, but people were able to catch it, and whenever you can catch a big bird like that, something's wrong. So, after years of being swanless, suddenly I had two. We didn't have to bring the second one inside the house at all because it wasn't as sick as Sabrina was. It did very well on the porch and provided company for Sabrina.

When her adopted family came to get her, I had mixed feelings about letting her go. I was happy to see her healthy and able to return to her pond, but I was going to miss her. Even though neither of us understood a word the other spoke, we communicated our pleasure in each other, and that's something most people can't seem to do.

"After what she's been through, you'd better herd her into your barn at night for the rest of the winter," I told the couple. As far as I know, that's what they did, and Sabrina had a complete recovery.

I don't always find out what happens to birds and animals after they leave here. Unless they get sick again, people seldom tell us about them. Sometimes all the animal or bird needs is nutrition, confinement, and protection for a while, and they'll heal themselves. But if they don't get help when they're in that kind of condition, they're dinner for somebody. That's the way this game is played.

I see so many animals that I can't always remember them individually. But I do remember Sabrina. There was something so special, so elegant about her. And after all these years I still remember her name. It was absolutely perfect for her. I mean, what other name but Sabrina would you give to a swan?

It's quiet at The Aark during the winter months. So much of nature is hibernating. Sometimes I feel as if I hibernate, too. The sense of anticipation that energizes me from early spring until late fall gives way to serenity. The volunteers are gone. The phone rings less often, and the calls are mostly from friends and family. The isolettes in the nursery are frequently empty. My lecture schedule begins to fill up, and there is work to be done around the house, but the rhythm of my life is less urgent and more predictable.

Ice is usually the reason we get calls for help in the winter. But most people don't realize that the problem isn't simply ice. If you're going to attempt a rescue, you have to give some thought to what may be under the ice. Is the water deep or shallow? Is it fairly still or is it moving? Sabrina was on a pond that was still and shallow, so while falling through the ice there was dangerous, it wasn't life-threatening—as long as the rescuers took reasonable precautions. When a river freezes over, that's something else.

About a year ago we had another unusually cold December. Temperatures were below freezing for days, and I had a few calls from people who saw waterfowl trapped in water that had frozen over. When I questioned them, it was obvious that a rescue would be too risky and very likely unsuccessful. One of the birds appeared to be dead, and I recommended that two others be shot by a conservation officer rather than let them starve to death.

At sundown on a Sunday afternoon, another call came in. It was from a young woman, and she was crying. "Is this The Aark Foundation?" she asked, although I had answered by announcing our name.

"Yes, may I help you?"

"Please, can you come out here?" she said. "There's a goose caught in the river!"

I asked her some questions, trying to calm her down. She told me she was a waitress in a restaurant on the bank of the Delaware River in New Hope. "There are all these Canada geese out here, and we feed them bread," she said. "This one—it's in trouble!"

"Well, we don't generally go out and get things," I told her. "If you can bring it to me, I'll be glad to treat it. We don't charge."

"I can't do that. It's out on the ice."

"How far out?"

"About twenty feet. It's frozen in the ice!"

"Tell me what you see—how do you know it's frozen?"

"This afternoon, when I went out to feed the geese some bread, this one didn't come in. I thought something was wrong, so I threw some pieces of bread right at it, and it went to fly up. But it couldn't fly. One leg is caught in the ice and it can't get out."

"That's not usually how birds freeze in," I explained. "Something else may be happening here. I don't know if there's anything I can do to help you."

She lost control of herself. "You mean you're just going to leave it there to die?" she said. She was starting to cry again. Her response was typical of most people when I can't help them. She immediately shifted all responsibility to me, and in her eyes it was my fault that the bird was going to die. I seemed inhumane because I couldn't do what she wanted me to do, and that made her angry. I understand. It hurts to stand by and see an animal suffer, and sometimes the only thing we can do is inflict part of our pain on someone else.

She was almost hysterical, and I was concerned about what she might try to do in an attempt to rescue the goose, so I kept talking to her. "I need to think about it," I said. "We don't have the equipment or the staff for a rescue, and this is not a simple matter of walking out there and getting the goose. The Delaware is a swift-moving river, and it's deep at that point. So please don't try to do something on your own. Twenty feet out on that ice is absolutely life-threatening."

"I wouldn't be alone," she insisted. "There are plenty of people here. They'll help me."

"Listen," I said, "I've got to tell you a few things about ice. If you go through it in deep water—and it's deep where you are—you can't be sure you'll come up where you went through. Chances are you'll come up under the ice, and if that happens, you're dead. You'll be swept along by the current and you'll never come up for air. If someone goes in after you, the same thing can happen to him."

For the first time she was silent.

"Give me a little time to figure out what we can do,"
I said.

"Okay," she said. But there was doubt in her voice.

"Give me your number and I'll call you back."

"You will?"

"I promise."

As I hung up, David, one of our volunteers, came in
to work in the nursery, which at that time was almost
empty. When I told him about the goose, he shook his
head. "Doesn't sound good," he said.

"I know," I agreed. "But I can't get that girl's voice
out of my head. It was full of tears."

For a while we considered some rescue operations, but
always there was the big question of what was underneath the ice. Finally I went to the phone and dialed the
number the girl had given me. "I can still hear her crying, David. I have to do something."

"Count me in," he said. David is strong and smart,
and I was glad to have him along.

The girl was so happy when I told her we would come
out and take a look at the bird. "It'll be dark by then,"
I told her, "so all we can do is look at the situation. We
can't actually do anything until daylight."

She understood.

On our way I shared my doubts about the bird with
David. "It can't have one leg frozen in," I said. "If that
were the case, it could still break free and fly. I think it's
something other than ice that's got hold of it."

"Like what?" David asked.

"Maybe monofilament," I said. Monofilament is a fish-
ing line, and it's very common for birds to get caught in
it. When a fisherman's line gets tangled in something,
he often cuts it and leaves it there because he's got plenty
more line on his reel and he doesn't want to spend time
unraveling knots. I fish, and I know how often the line
gets caught in something beyond my reach. But some
people give up too quickly. When they cut the line and
go, they don't realize that they've left a death trap for

some innocent creatures. The monofilament is thin, and the only way to break it is to cut it, so it lies there in the water waiting for something to swim by and get tangled up in it. It amputates the legs of birds; it strangles them; it traps them so that they can't get food leaving them to starve to death. We see a lot of these victims, and it's horrible. Most of it is inexcusable.

The more I thought about it, and the more I went over what the girl had described, the more I was convinced that the goose's leg was caught in something under the water. In that case, we would have to bring a cutting instrument with us when we went out on the ice to free the bird. That is, *if* we went out on the ice.

When we arrived at the restaurant it was dark. The girl had been watching for us and she came running out when she saw us drive up. She was young, maybe in her twenties, and pretty. Her eyes were red from crying and mascara was all over her face. "Oh, thank you, thank you!" she kept saying. "I can't believe you came! I was afraid you wouldn't bother."

A middle-aged man came out of the restaurant, and the girl introduced him as the manager. "This is the goose rescuer!" she told him, pointing to me. She was caught up in the excitement of a rescue operation. She still didn't realize that we were in real life, not a television adventure.

"I hope your customers don't know what's going on," I said to the manager. The last thing I wanted was a group of well-meaning people standing around telling me to do this and do that when they didn't know what was involved in the situation.

"No, I don't think so," the manager said. "I didn't want to get them upset so I didn't say anything."

"Good!"

They took us to the bank of the river and pointed toward the darkness. We used our flashlights to locate the goose and saw that its mate was nearby and able to move freely. It's almost impossible to determine the sex of geese, but they do form pairs and it was logical to assume that one was a male and one a female.

I snapped off my light. I didn't like what I saw. The goose was more than twenty feet out, and the ice was extremely unstable because the water under it was moving swiftly. In some places the ice had lifted up on itself. That's what happens when a river freezes over—the force of the water underneath the ice keeps breaking it and lifting huge portions up on top of ice that hasn't broken. The extra weight can cause more breakage, so you can't be sure the ice will stay where it is. When we tested it along the shore, the ice felt thick, but we couldn't be sure how thin it might be out where the bird was trapped.

I explained the situation to the girl. "I have to put a decent plan together before we can do anything," I told her. "We can't just charge out there and risk falling in. We also have to make sure that the bird is still alive when we go out. People risking their lives to save something that's already dead and can't be helped isn't very smart."

She was still very agitated, but she was sensible. She nodded her head in agreement.

"We'll come back tomorrow, when it's light," I said. "If we can't find a way to rescue the bird, I'll have it shot by a conservation officer. That's better than letting it suffer."

She took that well. "Okay," she said. "Just please do something. Don't leave it there." She looked tired. I wanted to put my arms around her and tell her everything was going to be all right, because that's what she wanted to hear. But I couldn't, because it wasn't true.

"We won't abandon it. I promise."

On the way back to The Aark, I remembered what Sabrina's family had done when they went out on the ice. "David," I said, "if we pushed a boat out there on the ice with us, we'd have something to get into if the ice started to come apart."

"I've got a canoe," he said. My first choice would have

been a rubber raft, but a canoe would do. Also, it was available, immediately.

"Will you bring it with you tomorrow morning?" I asked.

"Sure."

I hadn't even asked him if he wanted to go with me. I knew he would.

Early the next morning we were on the riverbank, and there was the goose, all by itself. Its mate had gone back to the shore, and that told me something: geese don't give up mates easily. The young woman was there and so was the manager and a few other employees. The restaurant wasn't open at that hour, so there weren't any customers around. The wind blowing in over the ice on the river made it colder than sin, but we were dressed for it. All that David and I could see of each other was our eyes. When we spoke, our words were muffled by collars zipped up to the bridges of our noses and scarves wound around our necks.

"I don't like the looks of this," David said. "You won't get more than a couple of feet out there unless you have some kind of spikes to keep you from sliding around in circles. Don't forget—you'll be pushing a canoe."

"How about those spikes they use for mountain climbing?" I suggested. "I know a store in Princeton that sells them."

"No—it won't work. Suppose you got out there and the ice broke. Suppose you got in the canoe and the ice broke some more. It could rock the canoe and push you under."

The canoe wasn't going to help. It would be more dangerous than going out with a rope around my waist. The goose hadn't made a sound in all that time. It was still alive, but it had to be very weak from its ordeal. My heart was out there with it.

For the rest of the day we explored all kinds of rescue possibilities, but none of them could overcome the risk

of the ice. The young woman went inside when the restaurant opened, but she kept coming out to see what
we were doing. She'd stand alongside us, listening and
shivering. I was almost as concerned for her as I was for
the goose because to her it must have seemed that we
weren't doing anything. Part of her understood what the
dangers were, but the rest of her didn't want to accept
them. She had stopped crying. I think she was out of
tears.

At sundown, David and I decided to leave because
there was nothing we could do in the dark. We knew
we were beaten, but we didn't want the young woman
to know it. Not yet. When we left, I told her to call me
first thing in the morning. "If the goose is still alive,
throw some bread at it. If it still can't fly, and if we
still can't think of a way to get out there, I'll call your
conservation officer. We won't let it starve."

She nodded sadly. "Anything's better than that," she
said.

She called me early the next morning. She sounded
relieved. "It's gone!" she said. "It must have gotten free
during the night! It must have flown away!"

She was happy and I wanted her to stay that way.
"Thank God!" I said, but I was thankful for the fact that
we didn't have to try to do anything else, because I knew
we couldn't. Yes, of course, the bird might have freed
itself and flown away, but I doubted it. Its leg definitely
was caught in something that wouldn't let go. What
probably happened was that the ice shifted again and
piled up on the goose, pushing it down under the water
and drowning it. I didn't tell that to the young woman.

"I want to thank you and David," she said. "You were
so wonderful to come out and try to help. We all thank
you."

"No, you're the one who's wonderful," I told her.
"You're very nice to care about a goose."

"Oh," she said, "anybody would."

"Not quite," I thought. Whoever cut some monofilament and left it there didn't even give a thought to a goose.

Fortunately, not all calls for help end in sadness. David and his sixteen-year-old son, Aaron, were here when another call came in. This time it was from a family who discovered an owl in their chimney. "We've got a wood-burning stove in our fireplace," the woman said, "but we're not using it now because we're afraid it might kill the owl. How can we get it out?" It was a few days after Christmas, and I was touched by a family that was willing to do without some heat to help a bird.

"What kind of an owl is it?" I asked her. "What did it look like?"

"I didn't see it," she said. "My son did. He says it's white. And it's big."

"Does it have a white, heart-shaped face?" I said.

"I'm not sure, and my son isn't here right now. But it's definitely white."

Big and *white* could have described a barn owl, and they're in trouble now because we've eliminated so much of their habitat. I decided to go out and see if I could help. David and Aaron wanted to come along.

"Okay," I said. "We need some heavy gloves, some rope, a box, and a good flashlight. And some jumpsuits." Whenever I have to go up a chimney, I always wear a World War II parachutist's jumpsuit. It's bright orange, and I've been told that it makes me look like something from outer space, but it does protect my clothing from the soot that comes pouring down once I start moving around in a chimney.

The address was about an hour's drive away. The man and woman met us at the door, wearing heavy sweaters. Looking past them I could see that the house was beautifully decorated for the holidays and absolutely immaculate, the kind of home that makes you scrape your shoes on the doormat even when you know they're perfectly clean.

In our orange suits we must have appeared a bit out of the ordinary, and the way the man looked at us confirmed it. But I reminded myself that the owl was the issue. "Can we pull your woodstove out of the fireplace?" I asked.

"Sure," the man said, "let me help."

We loosened a little soot by moving the stove. Being the smallest person present, I ducked and stuck my face and my flashlight up the chimney. I was appalled by what I saw.

"This is a fire waiting to happen," I said, backing out. "There's an awful lot of soot in this chimney. Have you ever had it cleaned?"

The man and woman glanced at each other briefly and shrugged.

"Please!" I said. "This has nothing to do with the owl. I'm concerned about *you*. All this soot is very dangerous. Please don't use your stove until you get this chimney cleaned!"

I knew what they were thinking. I remembered the way people used to behave when I lectured my parents' dinner guests about the environment and hunting. The woman wrung her hands and her husband rolled his eyes ceilingward as if he were thinking, "Get this broad outta here—she's a nut!" Aaron, in the meantime, had poked his head up the chimney and was met with a shower of ashes. I was wearing my glasses, but Aaron had no such protection and came away rubbing his eyes.

David has a good sense of timing. "Okay," he said, commandingly, "let's see what the problem is."

"You're too tall," I told him. "You can't fit in there. Let me go in."

I ducked and went back into the fireplace. Normally I can stand up inside a chimney, but this one was too narrow, and it was oddly shaped. Inside there were step-like shelves branching away and up from the opening. I had to stay crouched, but I switched on my flashlight and spotted the owl up on one of the shelves, just out of my reach. Usually, when an owl gets into a chimney, it lights on the damper and can't get up above it. All I have to do is reach in with my hand, grasp its feet, wiggle it around, and bring it down. But this little guy was so high up and the chimney was so narrow that I couldn't reach him. I could see that it was a screech owl, not a barn owl. They live in cavities, which is why they often end up in chimneys.

By this time my jumpsuit was no longer orange, but black with soot. There was no use trying to brush off the dirt because soot from a wood-burning stove is sticky. It adheres to clothing with a great determination. I wasn't concerned about how I looked, I just didn't want to dirty such a clean house.

"Do you have a mop?" I asked the woman. "Any kind—a dust mop, a floor mop?"

"Yes," she said and left. She came back with a string mop. I thought I could use it to extend the length of my arm and dislodge the bird from his perch. No such luck. Because of the peculiar design of the chimney I could lift the mop straight up, but I couldn't angle it over to the ledge where the bird was. The little guy was up there dancing around above me as if to say, "Catch me, catch me, if you can!"

"I've got an idea," David said. "Turn the mop upside down and I'll make a noose with something so you can drop it over the bird, tighten it, and pull it down." It was a brilliant suggestion! David made a loop out of the rope we had brought and fastened it to the mop handle so I could pull it tighter once I got it around the bird's body. Back into the chimney! Unfortunately, I still didn't have enough space to maneuver my arms well enough to get the loop over the bird, and the peculiar slant of the chimney defeated my efforts. Meanwhile I was dislodging storms of soot with the mop.

Then the man came up with an interesting suggestion: "Do you want to go up on the roof?"

David, being protective, said, "No, no, she doesn't want to go up on the roof."

"Wait a minute," I said. "Tell me about the roof."

The owner changed his mind. "No, *I'll* go up on the roof," he said. I understood how he felt. I'll go up on my roof, but I don't want anyone else doing it. If they do it wrong, either they'll get hurt or the roof will.

So I said, "Are you comfortable on your roof?"

He said he was.

"Okay," I told him. "I'll stay in the fireplace while you go up on the roof. Take a broom with you and lower it down the chimney. Maybe you can just brush it against the ledge and dislodge the owl. I'll be there to catch it."

"No problem," he said.

So there I was, in the fireplace, aiming my flashlight upward, and the man was up on the roof reaching down with a broom, and the owl was between us. The soot was coming down in showers because the man was loosening more of it with his broom. I had a better view of the bird, so I was directing the aim of the broom. "Come on, okay, go easy," I was telling him. "A little more to the left—no, back toward the right a bit—easy, easy." He was cleaning his chimney, whether he wanted to or not.

Like a shot, the little owl hopped onto the broom as it reached him and began to run up the handle.

"Bring him up, real slow," I called to the man on the roof. "Don't change your angle. Keep going—I can see it; keep going; pull it up!"

As the man pulled the broom up, the owl suddenly flew out of the chimney. I was afraid it would startle the man by coming up so fast and he might fall off the roof. "He's coming up!" I shouted. "Get your face away from the chimney—but don't lean back!"

Behind me, in the living room, I could hear the man's wife and David and Aaron yelling, "Yea! Go!"

The man was steady as a brick and got his face out of

the way without losing his balance as the owl flew up. We all gave him a cheer.

It was then that I saw what a mess we had made of a really lovely living room. There was soot all over the walls and the furniture. As we left in our not-so-orange suits, we tried to walk lightly so we wouldn't leave tracks, but the carpet was already dirt-colored. The nice thing about it was that the man and woman didn't seem to mind. Their faces were smeared with soot as they said good-bye, but they were smiling. They were happy that the owl got free. Some people are like that. They care.

6 / Building The Aark

I was not born with a head for business, nor did I seek that kind of knowledge as I grew up. If anything, I fought it. All I ever wanted was to be left alone to take care of my animals. Life, however, was much more practical. Through a series of events that seemed disastrous at the time, life forced me to realize that if I didn't have an organization behind me, I wasn't going to have any animals, either.

Before we became The Aark Foundation, Inc., my children and I always referred to ourselves as "the ark," because animals were in our home and part of our lives. Working with them was something I did out of love. I never expected to get paid for it. And because I considered my work a passion rather than a profession, other people did, too. They thought I was dedicated, self-sacrificing, noble, cute, and eccentric. Some of them could see that feeding my wild things cost me more money than I had, and they would reach down into their pockets and come up with a donation. Actually it was more of a handout because they were more concerned for me than for wildlife. I wasn't a legitimate organization that could go out and knock on doors, asking for contributions. Nor did I want to be. That seemed like nonsense. Anyone could see the kind of work I was doing—why did I need a brochure to describe it? I had better things to do with my time. So I paid for my animals' food and medication myself, and I paid taxes on the donations.

When we moved to Newtown, to the farm that became The Aark, I had to make a difficult decision. While I had enough land and buildings for my animals, I still didn't have enough time. I couldn't work full-time with my animals and full-time at the nature center, and I needed to earn some money because my trust fund didn't cover all my needs. I decided to give up my job and look for part-time work. I knew it wasn't going to be easy to get a job that fit into my schedule, but flexibility was an absolute necessity. All three girls were in school by then, but my patient load was increasing and I had baby birds and animals to feed every few hours.

I took several different jobs, and I enjoyed them all. I had had a few years' training in fashion design and designed and made my own clothes, so for a while I sold sewing machines and gave lessons in tailoring and dressmaking. For a year I worked with an upholsterer who was very understanding about all the times I had to dash home to feed my animals. But I had the most fun as a salesclerk in a men's haberdashery. I couldn't believe I was getting paid to help men look good. Sometimes a man would come in for a shirt, and I'd send him home with a three-piece suit, a shirt, socks, tie, and sweater—and he'd leave smiling. That job was a welcome change of pace for me. It was nice to make people smile and look better instead of dealing with matters of life and death.

But the jobs were jobs, nothing more. They helped me put food on the table. My real work was with the animals. Wherever I worked, I always made that very clear. "Look," I'd say, "I enjoy working here, but this isn't my main interest. It's not my career. I'm a hard worker and

I won't ever cheat you on time or energy, but, make no mistake, I don't intend to do this full-time. I just want to be able to feed my face and help my kids."

I didn't like seeing my daughters do without some of the things other kids took for granted. If there was a school dance, my girls didn't go because they didn't have the right clothes. School trips were out because we didn't have the money. But the girls never complained. Debbie had the hardest time because she was the oldest; I depended on her to help me with the ordinary chores that go into raising a family. But to a teenaged girl, household chores aren't ordinary. They keep her tied down. After school Debbie would clean and look after Sammy, who was then too young to be on her own. She'd help me feed the animals. She did her share of laundry, too. She didn't have much time for herself.

In those days, I was always worrying about getting enough money to buy food, not only for the animals but for ourselves. Heating our big house was more expensive than I anticipated, so I looked for ways to cut down on the amount of oil we burned. A woodstove helped. It was an ugly thing that took up the entire walk-in hearth in our living room, but it kept us warm. I managed enough to eat and the food was nutritious, but as hard as I tried to vary them, our meals were monotonous. To this day Debbie can't eat tuna fish because we ate it so often. Leah can't stand eggs for the same reason. But they were good, cheap forms of protein in our diet.

I found ways to cut down on the cost of the animals' food, too. When I learned that a nearby hatchery threw cockerels away, I asked the owners if we could have them, and they said yes. Cockerels are male chicks— baby roosters—and since one rooster can impregnate many hens, there isn't much of a demand for baby roosters. So most hatcheries kill most of them, disposing of them as soon as they hatch. My birds of prey could make better use of them. The only problem was that when the hatchery had some cockerels to give away, they wanted to get rid of them immediately. So they would call us and tell us to come and get them right away. Somehow the calls often came while the girls and I were eating dinner, and I'd have to drive over to the hatchery and bring home big plastic bags filled with dead cockerels. It was essential to freeze them as soon as possible, and later we would cut them up into pieces the birds could eat easily. So if we hadn't finished our dinner, we would push our dishes to one side, cover the other end of the table with newspaper, and get to work.

Leah still remembers that horrendous smell. "C'mon, Mom," she used to say, "can't we do this after we eat?"

"No, we can't," I'd tell her. "They'll go bad." I was very single-minded. It didn't bother me to eat with one hand and package dead cockerels with the other, and eventually it rubbed off on my daughters. Or, at least, on two of them. Sammy never approved. She found it disgusting. "Oh, Mom, this is awful!" she'd say.

I agreed with her. "It is," I said, "but it saves money."

"Just think of what we can buy with the money we save, Sammy," Debbie said. "More tuna fish!"

"Ugh!" was Sammy's only comment.

It seemed to me that I was struggling very hard and still not making enough money. Running back and forth between my jobs and my animals was taking too much of my time and energy, so I began to look for work I could do at home or something that allowed me to bring my animals with me. Housework seemed to be the perfect answer. I like to clean, and although some people consider cleaning other people's houses demeaning, I didn't. It paid well, I could set my own hours, and, assuming people were reasonable, I could take my patients along in my station wagon. Working two days a week, I would bring in the money I needed.

I had just about come to this conclusion when a couple who lived nearby brought me an injured bird. They had heard about my work, and when they saw the cages in my kitchen infirmary, they were fascinated. Their name was Purdy and they were delightful people. They knew very little about wildlife and asked all kinds of questions.

While I was examining the bird, they asked me whether I was paid for my work, and I said no. I told them I paid for the animals' food and medicine myself.

"Isn't that expensive?" Mrs. Purdy asked.

"It adds up," I said. "Right now I wouldn't mind having a little more money. In fact, I'm looking for some work cleaning houses. If you know anybody who needs a house cleaned, I'd appreciate it if you'd let me know."

Mr. Purdy smiled. "I can let you know right now," he said. "My wife needs someone to clean our house."

Mrs. Purdy hadn't missed the fact that my kitchen, cages and all, was immaculate. Was I grateful that I like a squeaky clean house and always kept mine that way! It was the best reference I could offer.

I worked for the Purdys and a few other people for several years. It was the perfect job for a rehabber. Animals that could feed themselves stayed home, but I brought my bottlefed babies with me because they had to be fed on schedule, every four hours. I carried them in a picnic basket with a lid on top and a heating pad inside. When I arrived at the Purdys, I'd put the basket on a kitchen counter and plug in the pad. Sometimes I had as many as six or eight squirrels and bunnies, and the Purdys loved watching me feed them. After a while I taught them how to do it and they helped. If their children were around, they always wanted to see the animals.

One day when I arrived, Mr. Purdy was about to dispose of a mouse he had caught in a trap. "Oh, don't throw it away!" I said.

"It's dead," he explained. He probably thought I wanted to turn the mouse into a patient.

"I know," I told him. "But it's such a waste to throw it away. I've got a red-tailed hawk that can eat it."

This was a side of rehabbing that the Purdys hadn't previously encountered. Some people might call it the gross side. I call it the food chain. Almost everything in nature is food for something or somebody else. Once you're able to accept that reality, once you're able to look at survival objectively rather than sentimentally, you can be more helpful.

Mr. Purdy was still holding the dead mouse by its tail. "Well, of course, you're welcome to it," he said, somewhat uncertainly. "Or, rather, your hawk is." Then he laughed. We all laughed. "Shall I wrap it?" he asked.

"Just put it in a plastic bag," I said. "And stick it in your freezer. I'll take it with me when I leave."

Mrs. Purdy had taken as much as she could. "The outside freezer," she said, tactfully, referring to the second freezer they kept on their back porch. She didn't want mice, in any form, in her kitchen.

From then on, Mr. Purdy would occasionally present me with a plastic big filled with frozen dead mice. After I stopped working for them, they would bring their children, and later their grandchildren, to The Aark to see our patients, and they always brought me their mice. They still do.

Cleaning houses gave me the money I needed for necessities, but we still couldn't afford extras. One Christmas there just wasn't enough money for a tree. "We're not going to have a tree this year," I told the girls. "I'm sorry, but that's how things are." Leah bit her lip, Debbie found something for Sammy to do—and I got busy with my patients. We all were hurting. As far as I was concerned, that was the end of it, but, kids being kids, I suppose the girls said something to their friends and the word got out that we weren't going to have a Christmas tree that year. On Christmas Eve day we had three—all of them dropped off by friends who wouldn't even stay long enough for us to thank them.

More than anything, though, Debbie wanted a horse. And we had the space for one. In those days, Newtown was farm country, and almost everyone had a horse. The neighborhood kids often rode to school on their horses, and I saw the way Debbie looked at them. I would have given almost anything to get a horse for her. But I couldn't afford to feed one, much less buy one.

What I needed was a free horse—and I got one! I heard that a boyhood friend of my brother was looking for a place to board his horse. His name was William Rossbauer—Billy, for short—and I had known him since I was a child. He used to be at all our family gatherings, but over the years I had lost touch with him. When I told him that I could take care of his horse but couldn't afford to feed it, we struck a deal.

"I'll pay for the feed and vet care," he said, "if you'll supply the stall and maintenance."

"Fine!" I said. Then I brought up the matter of Debbie. But not directly. "You live pretty far from us," I said, "so I gather that you won't be out to ride him very often."

Billy had done well in the home-heating business and didn't have much time off. "Unfortunately not," he said.

"Well, it's not good for a horse to be idle," I said, "so I wonder if you'd mind if my daughter Debbie rode him."

"Little Debbie?" he said, frowning.

"Little Debbie is going on thirteen, Billy. And she adores horses."

"My God!" he exclaimed. "There ought to be a law against time going so fast! *Thirteen!*"

"This is a very special girl, Billy. She'll take great care of your horse."

"Terrific!" he said.

A few days later Billy came out to look at our place and brought his horse with him. We loved the horse, but we didn't care much for his name. Billy called him just plain "horse," but since he was going to be part of our family we thought he ought to have a real name. We started calling him "Billy's horse," which very quickly became "Billy Horse" and stuck. He was a strikingly beautiful animal, a paint, with big orange patches on a white body, as if someone had splashed orange paint on him. His face was almost all white, with just one patch of orange, and he had one brown eye and one blue. The brown eye was in the orange patch and the blue eye was in the white part of his face. He was big, about seventeen and a half hands high—too high for Debbie to get on by herself. She didn't care. All she wanted to do was get up on Billy Horse and go. With Billy's help she did.

I couldn't believe how fast the two of them rode off. "Omigosh!" I thought. "There goes my child!" But I didn't say anything because I knew Billy wanted to see how Debbie handled the horse and I didn't want to embarrass her. They disappeared into the woods and didn't come back until a half hour later. "I can ride it! I can ride it!" Debbie was saying. Many years later Debbie told me that she didn't know how to ride. I assumed she did because she talked about horses so much. But she didn't want to give up her chance to have a horse, and she figured she'd work it out somehow. When she and Billy Horse started out that day, she didn't know how to turn around and come back. Obviously she learned.

"Can I have it?" she said. "Can I? Can I?" She was out of breath from exertion and excitement.

I looked at Billy and he nodded.

We didn't know it at the time, but that day was the beginning of two very important changes in our lives. Billy Horse came into Debbie's life at a time when a teenager wants to go her own way, and he made it possible for her to do it. She would come home from school, do her chores, see that Sammy was okay, and then get on Billy Horse and ride off. Sometimes she went to ride with her friends, sometimes she practiced the routines she and Billy Horse performed at shows, and sometimes it was enough for her just to be with him.

For all his size, he was a gentle animal. When he was in the barn, our chickens lived in the loft over his head and they often laid their eggs in his stall. When he went to sleep, the chickens would lie between his legs, and when he wanted to get up he would bump them gently so they would get out of his way and not get hurt. There were always at least two nests in his stall, and he never broke an egg or stepped on a chick.

Billy Horse was with us for a long time and lived to a very old age. We never were sure how old he was when we got him because he didn't have papers. But when he died, the vet said that, judging by his teeth, he appeared to be about thirty-two years old.

The other change in our life was Billy Rossbauer's involvement in my work. He was the one with the business mind, and he was appalled by my attitude toward money. Eventually he was to change the way I thought about my work and teach me how to do it more effectively. But I fought him most of the way.

"You mean you carry all this yourself?" he said when he started helping out in the nursery. "You pay for it out of your pocket?"

"Well, some people give donations," I said.

"But you're counting that as personal income," he said. "You're paying taxes on it. That's crazy!"

He said something about setting up a nonprofit organization, and that was when I stopped listening. I didn't like that kind of talk. I had known other rehabbers who incorporated and set up boards of directors, and the next thing you knew they were out on their ears. I didn't want a board or anyone else telling me what to do. I assured Billy that I was doing just fine, thank you.

Then I woke up one morning and looked out my bedroom window and saw some orange-tipped stakes in a field down the road where my nearest neighbor's property met mine. They were surveyor's stakes. New houses were going up. I didn't know how many, but it didn't matter. I felt as if my world were crashing in on me. Until then there was nothing but cornfields between me and a state park a couple of miles away. I couldn't see my neighbors' roofs or smell their barbecues or hear their children, and that, to me, is the only way for people to live. I could release my animals, knowing they were going back into the wild, not into somebody's yard. When animals and birds are first released, they're not as wary as they will be in a few more days. The only things they had to contend with on our land were God, the sky, and natural predators. But man would be a far greater threat to them. At that time I was treating about three hundred patients a year. What would all these new homebuyers think about wildlife? Would they consider them pests?

I was scared that the builders were going to cut down all the hedgerows and level the land so there wouldn't be any habitat left. In my mind's eye, I could see hordes of people encroaching on our woods, our streams, our pastures. I panicked. For some reason I felt like one of those old-time cavalry officers being stripped of his buttons and gold braid. Every time I looked at those orange-tipped surveyor's stakes, I felt another button got ripped off.

That was a bad week. A few days earlier I had lost a precious friend. She was a big white barnyard goose—the image of Mother Goose—and I had had her since my first year at the farm. She was also the first goose that was friendly, and from the moment we met she followed me everywhere. I didn't have as many animals then, and I had more time to spend with her. A family brought her in to me, hoping I could place her in somebody's barnyard because they couldn't take care of her anymore. They had found her when she was a chick, and she was so cute they tried to raise her as a family pet. They didn't realize that when geese grow up, they can be pretty undesirable in a suburban setting. They're an easy prey for dogs that aren't on a leash, and their excrement is messy. They really belong in a barnyard.

I get a lot of calls from people who find young ducks and geese, especially along the Delaware River canal. They think that because they find the babies in the woods, they're wild. But they aren't. They're born to ducks and geese that escaped from a barnyard or to baby fowl people buy at Easter and then release because they don't know what to do with them once they grow out of the fuzzy stage. These birds mate and hatch eggs, but they don't do well as parents: they aren't wild birds, and they belong in a barnyard situation where they're fenced in and fed. Fighting the environment, protecting themselves, and trying to keep tabs on a lot of babies all take too much out of them. Consequently, their babies stray and get separated from their parents, and that's when people find them. Usually people don't realize that they're domestic fowl and can't survive free. So I always try to find a barnyard situation for them because that's where they have a better chance for a normal life.

I kept the goose the family brought me because we had a barnyard; and she was so accustomed to being around people that she was super friendly. We became best friends.

At night I barn my chickens, ducks, and geese to protect them, because to 'coons and foxes an open barn is a takeout restaurant. Many of our local predators are animals I have worked on, and they're welcome guests outside at night, but not in my barn. I put table scraps out for them so they're less likely to help themselves to the living, and I keep looking for better ways to make the barn safe, but they fiddle with locks and doors and often find ways to break in. It takes a long time to make a barn tight, and we've had our share of things that were donated to the cause of keeping Old Mama Fox and Old Daddy 'Coon alive.

A few days before I saw signs that new houses were going up, I went to the barn in the morning to open it up, and I found my lovely goose lying on the floor, all bloody and torn. She was still alive, but barely. I picked her up and started carrying her to the infirmary but I could see she wasn't going to live. I also knew I couldn't bring myself to put her down. I sat down in the driveway, holding her in my arms, rocking her and pressing my head against her. I had her blood all over me, so

when a friend of mine drove up she thought something
had happened to me. She got out of her car and ran to
me, but as soon as she saw my goose she understood.
She knelt down and put her arms around me. I shrugged
her off.

"No!" I said, and she let go as if I had hit her. I didn't
want to be comforted. I didn't want to explain how I felt.
I was enraged at the uselessness of death and the brutal-
ity of nature. I had seen so many animals die and I
thought I was hardened to it because I didn't react. Then,
suddenly, something close to me died, and it was as if
all the deaths were happening again. I could feel each
one of them. As I sat there in the driveway, crying, I
was mourning the dear goose now dead in my arms, but
I was also mourning every single animal I had watched
die. And there was no comfort for such a loss.

A few days later, on the morning I saw the stakes
down the road, I was opening the barn door and wondering how much longer I would be able to do it. I was
thinking, "How can I deal with so many people around
me? It won't be safe for the animals. I'll have to close
down!"

I was so depressed that I couldn't conceal it. I was
expecting a visit from a woman named Charlotte Dyer,
who was said to be very wealthy and interested in conservation. She had heard about my work as a rehabber
and wanted to look over my facilities. I knew it was
important for me to meet her, but at that point I didn't
think I would have the farm much longer.

When she arrived she certainly didn't fit the stereotype
of a rich woman. She was dressed simply in jeans, a
faded plaid shirt frayed at the cuffs, and well-worn boots.
She was a few inches taller than I am and stood very
straight, which made her appear quite tall. She had an
athletic, muscular body. She was in her sixties, but
looked younger. Her long, thin face with bright blue eyes
had a strong kind of beauty.

She saw that something was wrong and, being a very

direct woman, she asked me, "What's got you so upset?" She had been an army major in World War II and was retired. When she spoke, she was still a major and the rest of the world were privates, so when she asked a question, people answered. I told her about my goose and about my fear that I wouldn't be able to stay at the farm.

We were standing near one of the flight pens behind the house, and I had explained how I released hawks. "It took me years to find this place," I said, "but, as you can see, I need a lot of space to make things work right."

She told me she lived up on Jericho Mountain, near New Hope, Pennsylvania; I had heard about the beautiful big farm she owned. "Let's set a time for you to come see where I live," she said. "I think you'll like it."

Like it? I loved it! It was vast. The land, the houses, everything about it was exquisite. And it was all by itself. The house was similar to the one we were living in, although not quite as large. The barns were good and sound, and behind one of them was a building that housed an office, a meeting room, and a library-lecture room. I don't know how many acres there were, but they stretched on forever. I saw two ponds, some woods and fields, all of it meticulously maintained.

Charlotte was very proud of it. She told me she and her husband lived there all year round. They had no children. As she marched ahead of me, she kept saying, "Could you use a building like this?"

"Oh, yes!" I told her. "I could move my infirmary out of the kitchen if I had a building like this."

"Would this work for you?" she asked when she switched on the lights in the lecture room.

"It would be wonderful!" I said. "I'm always going out to do programs at schools and civic groups, but with a room like this I could do programs right on the spot."

Charlotte drew herself up and issued a command. "Well, then," she said, "put a proposal together! How long do you think that will take you?"

I was stunned. I didn't know what she was getting at, and I didn't know what a proposal was or what it had to do with wildlife. When I hesitated, she became impatient. "I want to give you this farm," she explained. "My husband and I don't have any heirs, and this place is very dear to us. I don't want it going to just anybody. I want it to serve a purpose, to do some good. Is that clear?"

"Yes!" I said, but that wasn't quite true. At that moment, nothing was clear. Only a few days ago I thought I was losing my home. Now this woman I hardly knew wanted to give me hers.

She snapped off the light in the lecture room and led me outside. "Now, you'll have to get started on that proposal," she was saying. "What we'll need is a five-year projection of your rehabilitation program . . . and then. . . ." I wasn't hearing her.

I called Billy as soon as I got home. "I don't know what she's talking about!" I told him. "I think she wants to give me this gorgeous piece of the world, but I'm not sure. You understand this kind of thing, so please, explain it to me!"

"Calm down," he said. "It's all very logical. I'll drive out tonight and we'll talk about it."

By the time he arrived I was even more upset. "What's this business about a five-year projection?" I said. "Good God, I can barely feed my animals! Would you like to hear what my proposal is? I'll give it to you in a few words: I'll do this work until I drop, every day for the rest of my life. *That's* my proposal!"

"MJ, don't complicate things," Billy said. "This is normal business procedure. A five-year projection is a formality. You can hire someone to write it up for you. It simply states, in detail, how you plan to expand your work over the next five years." I couldn't believe it. He didn't even sound like Billy. He sounded like a recording.

"Before you do anything, though, you've got to make

The Aark a non-profit foundation." When I glared at him, he held up his hand. "Let me finish," he said. 'If you're a non-profit foundation, you can ask people to donate money to support your work. You can go to corporations and ask for donations. You'll be legitimate. And you won't have to pay taxes on the money you get. You'll be able to take a salary—and maybe pay a few assistants. And you'll be able to accept Charlotte Dyer's gift, free of charge."

At last I was hearing what Billy had been telling me for a long time. Maybe it was the surveyor's stakes and my fear of losing the farm that did it. If that's true, then I'm grateful, because it forced me to realize that I couldn't just stay out of people's sight and do my work. I had to become visible. I had to learn how to advertise what I was doing.

"Okay," I said, with a long, slow sigh. "What do I have to do?"

"Get the legal work done. See your lawyer."

"I don't have one. I can't pay for one—you know that."

"Never mind," he said. "Go to my lawyer and I'll pay for it."

"I'm a proud woman, Billy," I said. "I can't do that."

"Yes, you can. Damn it, MJ, can't I give a gift to The Aark?"

I was too choked up to say anymore. I knew he was right, but his gift was more than generous. He was the first person to back up my work with his money as well as his belief in it. He wasn't giving me a handout. He was standing behind what I did. I could accept that. But I couldn't find the words to tell him what it meant to me.

A few weeks later Billy showed up unexpectedly. "Come out to the road," he said. "I've got something to show you."

My driveway is a half mile long, so we drove out in his car. At first I didn't see anything. Then I did. At the entrance to the driveway, on the right side, was a sign, THE AARK.

Neither of us said a word. Billy was waiting for me to speak, and I didn't know what to say—because I absolutely loathed the sign. It was a cutesy sort of thing, with letters in imitation gold and a silly little roof over it. I somehow thought that if I ever had a sign, it would be subtle and classy, and this one wasn't. I also resented the fact that Billy had chosen it without even consulting me. I blew up. "That's horrible!" I said, clenching my teeth.

"I had it made for you!" he said.

"I don't give a damn! Take it down!"

"Look, it didn't turn out quite the way I wanted it, but you need a sign."

"Not that one. It's a piece of shit." I got out of his car and trudged back down the driveway. I didn't even want to share the same car seat with him.

Billy didn't come back that day. Later, when I drove to the feed store to pick up some supplies, I didn't see the sign and thought he must have taken it with him. Then I saw it lying in the grass and got out of the car to pick it up. Someone had hacked at it with an axe and knocked some pieces off. But the name was intact. When I saw it lying there, wounded, I felt tears come to my eyes. Poor Billy! The sign wasn't what he wanted it to be, either, but he wanted to give me something that made The Aark official—and I didn't know how to receive it graciously. I picked up the sign and scrounged around for all the missing pieces. I took them home with me and put the sign back together as well as I could. It was still a tacky work of art, but I was learning to love it. Eventually Billy had another sign made, something more tasteful, but the original one hangs high up on my barn and has aged with some distinction. Whenever I'm feeling a little down because things aren't going my way, I go outside and look at it. Most times it makes me feel better.

I didn't get the farm on Jericho Mountain because I couldn't put a proper proposal together. I still couldn't accept the need for one: if Charlotte Dyer wanted to give me some of her property, why couldn't we just shake hands on it? If we trusted each other, what more did we need? I was already very nervous and uncertain about heading a foundation, and that was about all the business education I could handle at the time.

Charlotte was disappointed, but she couldn't make an exception in my case. She had offered the property to others and they had submitted proposals and five-year plans. She couldn't understand why I was so stubborn. Looking back, neither can I. I suppose I just hadn't grown up enough. Today I hire people to write proposals for The Aark because I recognize the need for them. When you get right down to it, they're bullshit, nothing more. They don't change the kind of work we do or how we do it. They have nothing to do with our integrity or our intentions. They're simply a bunch of magic words that open doors to the money our animals need.

In the long run, Charlotte's gift, even though we didn't get it, was a turning point for The Aark because it motivated me to get incorporated. And what a difference an *Inc.* makes! Now when we ask for donations, we present financial statements. We spell out how much money comes in and how we spend it. We describe how we want to grow and why. *Inc.* means that The Aark is a reality rather than my private passion, and people have to deal with it as a reality. We can say that we're a nonprofit organization and people respond with, "Well, they must be okay." And we are.

Inc. also meant that we could accept donations without paying taxes on them, that I could take a small salary for myself whenever we could afford it. Instead of looking for part-time jobs, I could devote all my energy to the animals. As our patient load increased, I was able to hire a part-time staff to work with me.

I had dreaded having to answer to a board of directors

because I thought they wouldn't understand my work and would try to change the way I did it. Then I realized that directors were supposed to help me, not get in my way, so I chose men and women who had put in active time at The Aark, people who knocked on doors and asked for money or rolled up their sleeves and got their hands dirty. I don't ask people to sit on my board unless I've known them and worked with them for a couple of years, and I've never been turned down when I ask someone to serve. Our board members know what our problems are and they want to help us to solve them. "This is a dictatorship," I tell them. "If you don't like it, then don't sit on my board. This is my baby, my rehab license, and it's my way. I'll sit through any discussion you want to have, and if you can present good reasons why we should do something or change something, I'll do it. But when I say, 'That's it, here's what we're going to do,' that's the end of the discussion." We've worked well together.

After we became an *Inc.*, my patient load more than tripled and I treated over one thousand animals and birds in our first year. And we kept on growing. Part of the increase came from our visibility as a non-profit organization. The rest came from my neighbors, the people I thought were going to make my life miserable.

In all fairness to the developer, he was considerate and left the hedgerows intact. He also left a good buffer of trees between The Aark and the main road. There was a red-tailed hawk's nest up in one of those trees, and it's still there. The houses are lovely and quite far apart, and the people who moved into them were environmentally educated. They got to know us because their children were interested in our work and brought them in to see it. Not one neighbor cut down a tree or a thorny bush to clear the view because they know that wildlife needs such things.

I don't have to patrol the borders of my property anymore, looking for poachers. My neighbors do that with

A handsome young red fox. *(Photography by Ted Cooper.)*

all My Love,
Merry Christmas
1976
Jim

Precious during the hunting season. We tied ribbons around her neck, hoping hunters would respect the fact that she was hand-raised. *(Photography by Jim Williams.)*

A basket serves as a nest for great-horned owl babies. *(Copyright © Joni Ludlow, photographer.)*

Paul K. Thomas, a volunteer and board member, feeds a baby groundhog in the Intensive Care Unit. You can see two of our incubators in the background. *(Photography by Noreen Pallanta.)*

Our bathtubs serve many purposes. Here one is a
pond for a pied-billed grebe.

Me with Zorie, a fruit-eating bat in the custody of
Dr. Merlin Tuttle, world-renowned authority on bats.

The crew after we completed our Christmas capture of a red-tailed hawk. *(Photography by Diane Nickerson.)*

Donald watches as I release a red-shouldered hawk.

A Northern Harrier spreads its wings and tail on my fist. Notice the jess on the leg.

A red-shouldered hawk in a flight pen.

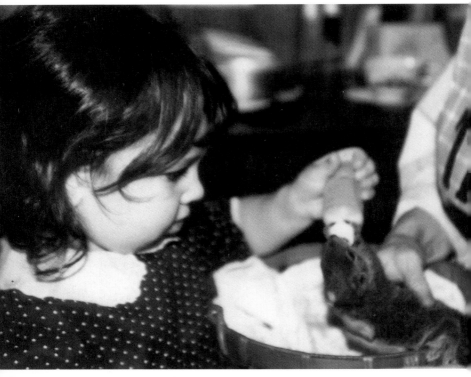

At the age of three, my granddaughter Rebecca was already proving to be a valuable assistant. Here she is in the nursery, feeding a baby squirrel.

such determination that no poacher gets past them. As they began to see how much harm pesticides and herbicides can do to birds and animals, they started feeding their lawns organically.

Now, when I talk to young people who want to be rehabbers, I tell them that it's okay to be idealistic. In fact, they have to be, because the material rewards in this business are few. But I try to remind them that wildlife rehabilitation *is* a business, and if they want to do well by the animals, they had better get some business sense into their heads.

To some degree I still fight the administrative demands in my work. I'm afraid of getting lost in them. But in a way that fear may serve as an advantage, because it prevents the paperwork from gobbling me up. It's hard for me to be working with babies in the nursery when I know I should be on the phone making speaking arrangements and setting dates for programs. But at least now, I know I'll eventually get to the phone. It's a matter of timing: babies can't wait; the phone can—does.

7 / Precious

I drive very slowly when I turn into my driveway after dark, because it's not unusual to see a herd of deer ahead of me. I always turn off my lights, roll down my window, and talk to them softly as I inch past them. Although I can't tell one from another, I'm sure that some of them came to The Aark as fawns and were released when they were old enough to take care of themselves. I often wonder if, in some way, they remember me.

One night I came upon ten deer grazing along the driveway, and they started to run away as my car approached. Even though it was the right thing for them to do, I couldn't help myself. "Hey, you!" I called after them. "I've had my hands on half of you! I helped you stay in this world. I touched you. I fed you. I wiped your bottoms! Where are you going?"

All ten of them stopped. That had never happened. In the moonlight I could see them looking back at me. A few took a step toward me as if to say, "Is that you, Mom?" Then they turned and went their way, but slowly this time, grazing as they went. In that instant of hesitation I felt as if they were acknowledging my part in their lives, and I almost cried. I drove carefully, staying to one side so I wouldn't alarm them. "Thank you, God, thank you!" I said. I have never been able to take such things for granted.

In the spring, in May when does are giving birth, people bring us fawns. Most of them are found along Swamp Road, a busy two-lane road with high embankments and fields on each side. Usually the fawns are only a day or two old, and my guess is that they were born in the fields close to the embankment and then tumbled down onto the road because they weren't steady on their feet yet. Sometimes people find them in a field where the mother may have left them while she went to graze. Normally the baby will stay there, absolutely still, until the mother comes back to nurse it. Staying still is a fawn's only defense against predators, and at that early age it doesn't have a scent. But people can walk right up to a fawn and pick it up, which they do all too often. They mean well, but they don't know how to look for signs of the mother before they move the fawn. If they don't see her, they assume she isn't there.

Whenever possible, we try to put a fawn back where the mother can find it. Of course, if the mother was seen dead on the road, or if the fawn was found by the body of a dead doe, then the fawn should be sheltered. And if we can't tell which field is the right one, then we don't try putting it back. But if the fawn was found in a field, and if we can find the right one, then the chances are good that its mother will come back for it.

One day a man came in with a fawn that was only hours old. He was very excited. "Look at this little thing!" he said. "Can you do something for it?"

I examined the fawn and found no wounds or broken bones. It was hardly more than a handful. Its fur was the color of real honey before it gets processed and commercialized—a rich reddish-brown—and it had cream-colored spots on its back. The eyes were black-blue, and its black nose was shiny-wet with inquisitiveness. Its hooves were soft, and it teetered on slender legs that hadn't yet gained the strength to support its body. It looked like a new ballerina, up on its toes and a bit wobbly on them. As far as I could see, the animal was healthy.

I asked the man where he found it. He described a stretch along Swamp Road, across from a horse farm. I knew the area.

"Was there any sign of a deer in the road?" I asked him. "A dead one?"

"No. Just this little thing, all by itself, off on the shoulder."

"I'd like to try putting it back," I said. "Will you show me where you found it?"

"Sure," he said. "But can you just leave it there? Won't something happen to it? Suppose the mother doesn't come back?"

They were normal, logical questions, and I assured him we wouldn't abandon the fawn. "First we'll take it back to where you found it and look for a field. If I can find a deer path in the field, we'll put the fawn there and leave. Does don't stay with their fawns all the time. They have to leave them to eat so they can nurse their young.

"We'll go back around midnight to check on the fawn," I assured him. "If the mother came back for it, it may be gone. But if the fawn wandered off again, it won't go far and we'll find it. If the mother hasn't come back—if something happened to her so she can't come back—we'll know."

"How?" he asked.

"This baby's only a few hours old. It needs a lot of milk. If the mother doesn't come back to nurse it by midnight, the fawn will look a bit emaciated."

"And you'll bring it back here?"

"Absolutely."

We took the fawn with us. It didn't protest; it was warm and perfectly content. We drove to the spot along

Swamp Road where the man had found it, and the embankment was like a wall rising straight up from the road. Unfortunately it was decorated in poison ivy, but up we went, grabbing at the weeds for support. When we got to the top we found a hedgerow of thorny bushes and trees. Beyond it we saw a lovely field. It was exactly where a fawn should be.

I'm accustomed to looking for a deer run, and I found one not far from some woods at the far end of the field. The fawn didn't resist when we left it there, but the man was anxious. "You're sure it'll be okay?" he said uneasily.

"I can't guarantee there isn't a fox in the area," I told him. "But we can't take all the risks out of life. If we can get this baby back to its mother, that's its best chance."

"I guess so," he said, but I knew he wasn't happy with my decision. "I'd like to come back with you tonight—if that's all right with you."

"Fine!" I said. He was nice. Some people wouldn't have been willing to give up their time.

It was a little after midnight when we went back, and by then I knew that we shared a bad case of poison ivy. Using our flashlights we followed the deer run back to where we had left the fawn. We could see where it had lain, waiting, because the grass was pressed down, and there were signs that the mother had come to the spot. I could see tracks where the two of them had gone off in another direction, back toward the woods and away from the road. Just to be sure, we searched a wide area around us and found nothing.

"How can you be sure it's all right?" the man asked me. I'm often asked that question.

"I can't," I said. "I can't really be sure you're going to get home tonight, either, but that's not my responsibility."

He nodded, but I think he was a bit uncomfortable with my point of view. Some people are. They can't understand how I can love an animal and let it go. But I believe that loving wild things means letting them go. We don't have the right to hold onto them.

I learned that lesson back in 1976 from a doe that was brought to me when she was a day old. She was my first fawn, and it was my first year as a full-time rehabber. A game warden found her on a road, and when he handed her to me he said, "Call her Precious—she's so precious!" I couldn't resist her or the name. I knew a lot about deer, but I had never raised a fawn, so she was not only adorable but fascinating. I carried her under my arm with one hand under her chest so that her legs could dangle free. Fawn legs should never be restricted because they're very fragile. If you hold their legs tightly when they want to kick out, they'll kick out anyway and might break a leg. So you have to be sure their legs are free to move when you pick them up. If they kick you, that may be a little rough on you, but at least their legs won't get hurt. Another way to hold a fawn is to put your other hand under its bottom, but you won't like what happens: as soon as you touch their behinds, you stimulate them and they either pee or poop. Usually I carry them with one hand and let their behinds hang out the back. They pee and poop down my leg, but in my line of work you get used to it.

I hadn't intended to call her anything, except perhaps "Little One," a name I use for many animals. But since she was my first fawn, I fussed over her and did some things I wouldn't do now. Besides, I don't know anyone who can keep her hands off a fawn. From the beginning Precious was friendly and affectionate. She let me hold her face to help her drink from her bottle, and not all fawns will do that. Her fur at that young age was longer and softer than the fur of a full-grown doe because it was meant to keep her warm. It was fuzzy, too, and wherever she licked herself she left unruly little cowlicks that I simply had to touch. She was all ears and eyes when she looked at me, and if I put my head close to hers, I got kissed. Fawns like to lick the salt off your skin, so if you're within range, that's what happens. I can assure you, when you're depressed there's nothing in the whole universe better than fawn kisses to make you feel better. Nothing! If I could bottle them, I'd be a millionaire.

Today, when fawns come in, we put them in a playpen or let them loose in the office for a few days. If they're in a playpen, they learn how to jump out very quickly. They're not steady on their legs yet, and they slip on the vinyl tile, so we put mover's quilts on the floor. We didn't use play pens when we had Precious; instead, we kept her in the kitchen for about five days until she learned to identify us as a source of food. She made herself comfortable in a corner out of the way, and when the girls and I called her, she would come to us, still teetery on her long slender legs, eager for her bottle. Fawns drink a lot of milk. For the first five days we have them, while they're in the nursery, we give them as many as five bottles a day, and these bottles hold two quarts. In the wild, the deer mothers don't feed their fawns frequently and usually let them tank up when they do, so we let them nurse the same way. Once we let the fawns go free, we feed them on demand, which is usually about two or three bottles a day. Very quickly they get down to one bottle, and then none.

After a few days Precious began to follow us outside. We let her come along, but the girls and I took turns walking with her so she wouldn't wander off and get lost. She was still tiny and there were foxes in the area. Our inexperience made us overprotective of her because we didn't know what to expect. But she got away from us anyway. We'd see her one minute and she'd be gone the next. She was so beautifully camouflaged that we would walk right past her without seeing her. Then suddenly she'd show up again.

Finally I began to realize that she was the teacher and we were the students. "We're going to do things her way," I told the girls. "We'll put her out in the morning, and we *won't* stay with her." Of course, I worried about her. I had handled her so much that I was bonded to her. She was becoming like one of my dogs, a member of the family. I kept reminding myself that she wasn't domesticated and would have to be released, but my heart wasn't listening to what my head was saying. After I put her out each morning, I was uneasy until she came back for food. I always fed her at the same door, and she'd come in and stand there, hollering and kicking the door, when she was hungry for her bottle. Deer make a bleating sound, like sheep, but sometimes louder, and I was always relieved when I heard her. By the time she was a month old she had dropped down to two bottles a day, and she'd wander off again as soon as she finished them.

We'd see her, though. Sometimes Debbie caught glimpses of her when she rode Billy Horse, and when the girls were playing Precious would come out of the bushes to join them. She loved games. She used to walk in the hayfields on either side of the house, and she blended in so well we couldn't see her. If a storm was coming, I'd go out to look for her because I didn't want her out there in severe weather. When the wind is just right and the rain is heavy, whole sections of a hayfield will go down flat, and if a fawn gets trapped under that weight it can drown. I was also concerned because fawns are terrified of thunder and lightning. They'll run in any direction, crashing into trees and fences, and they can hurt themselves badly.

One day when a storm was coming and I was out in the fields calling "Precious! Precious!" at the top of my lungs, I came across two does and several fawns. I had stumbled into a wild deer nursery and birthing area, so I backed out as fast as I could. I didn't have a chance to see whether one of the fawns was mine—and when fawns are that young, you can tell yours from another—

but I decided that if Precious was in there, she was in good company.

I was almost back at the house when the storm hit with a roar of thunder. Behind me I heard a high-pitched bleating and turned to see Precious come charging out of the field toward me. I opened the back door, called "Precious!" and she bolted into the house ahead of me.

At night we made more of an effort to find her and bring her into the house because I was afraid of foxes. But I made a mistake in doing that because I conditioned her to come inside at night and that isn't the natural way of deer. They're nocturnal animals. And eventually Precious let me know that she wasn't like a dog or a cat. She wanted to be free.

For a while she was half pet, half wild thing. She loved to play with the children and she'd let them dress her up like a doll. She got along very well with my dogs, but when another dog came onto the property she disappeared. Fortunately she knew the difference. But she began to resist us a little more as time went on. She was away longer, sometimes for more than a day. She was growing up and was too big for us to pick up and put down, so she was able to go her own way. She was off her bottle but she came in for treats. I used to carry granola cookies in my pocket just in case she showed up. Sometimes she'd follow the kids into the house after playing with them, and I'd find her asleep on the sofa.

I made a point of telling the children not to bring her in on one special occasion. I was getting serious about a man I was seeing, and I had invited his parents to dinner. I knew they were a little skeptical of my work, and they weren't particularly comfortable with me, so I went all-out to make it an absolutely perfect evening.

The dining-room table looked exquisite. I used my great-grandmother's lace tablecloth, my Lenox China, my crystal, and my sterling. I had bought an arrangement of flowers for a centerpiece. My children looked exquisite.

Sammy was eight, Leah was twelve, and Debbie was sixteen, and they wore long skirts and blouses, which was the style then. They were dressed on time, too. Now it was my turn to get exquisite. I was planning to wear a long pleated plaid skirt and a dark green velvet jacket. This was going to be a class affair. "Don't let that fawn in the house. And no raccoons. Please, not today!" I had told the girls.

"If they arrive before I come down, let them in," I said as I went upstairs. "Start serving the hors d'oeuvres— they're in the refrigerator. And be polite!"

I was almost ready to come downstairs when I heard ominous sounds. My children were whispering too loud, and all I could make out was *"Don't tell Mom!"* I came down the stairs quietly, to see what was going on. If it wasn't something serious, I was going to let it go this one time.

The girls were squeezed into the dining-room doorway, staring at something. They didn't move as I came up behind them. Then, when I looked past them, I froze. There, on top of my exquisite table, was Precious, munching my flower arrangement. She must have jumped up, but she hadn't knocked anything over. It was as if some invisible force had lifted her up by invisible strings and put her down in the middle of my formal settings.

I didn't dare move or utter a sound. If I called her, I could just imagine her scampering around, getting her hooves caught in the lace tablecloth, and scattering everything off the table. I was frantically trying to figure out how I could get her off without exciting her so that at least some of my china and crystal—and, I hoped, my great-grandmother's tablecloth—could be saved.

Precious lifted her head and looked at us. Perhaps she decided that playing with the girls would be more fun, and she picked her way through glasses and plates with delicate ease and jumped off the table. There wasn't even a wrinkle in the tablecloth! The only sign that she had been there was my flower arrangement: It was nothing but stems. "Get that fawn out of here—NOW!" I said in the kind of voice mothers use when they mean "Do it!"

I could guess what had happened. The girls were so accustomed to inviting Precious into the house to play that they forgot my warning. We got off easily, but I was learning another lesson about raising a fawn: once it connects you with food and wants to go outdoors, you don't bring it into your house. If you do, the time will come when you'll have to stop, like it or not, because you and your wild creature will be getting in each other's way. It was that time for us. I knew better than to try to make a pet out of Precious, and I wasn't willing to go wild.

Our dinner that evening was memorable in another way as well. After our guests arrived, it became clear that they did not approve of my work with wildlife. They were openly critical of the fact that animals lived in our house—that some were in the kitchen while I was preparing food! My daughters—usually not rambunctious children but dependably well-behaved—are very loyal to me, and they took offense at our guests' remarks.

Later, while we adults were sitting over coffee, discussing animals, the girls went upstairs—to bed, I thought. The conversation between my friend's mother and me was becoming a bit heated when I suddenly thought I noticed something coming down from the ceiling. Was it water? No, it couldn't be.

But it was. Drops of water were falling onto my friend's mother's head and shoulders. Occasionally, she shook her shoulders, as if brushing away an annoying insect, but she went right on telling me why it was wrong to live among animals. It was dirty, she said, unhealthy.

I looked up. Above her head was a small knothole in one of the ceiling's exposed beams, going through to the wood floor above the dining room. I knew it was there. So did my daughters. And I realized instantly that the girls were up there, dropping water on our guest's head. Shortly after I looked up, the dripping stopped. Our guest never caught on.

Precious was a lovely young doe with sleek taupe fur when the hunting season arrived, and even though we used to patrol our land on horseback, poachers still got in. I was sick at the thought that Precious might be shot. I tried to keep her close to home until February, when the season was over. At night I would coax her into the barn with treats. To protect her in daylight I spray-painted a big ABSOLUTELY NO on her sides, but she licked it off. So we tied ribbons around her neck to notify hunters that she was a hand-raised animal and to warn them off shooting her. There was a danger in the ribbons, too, because if they got caught on something she could have hurt herself trying to pull free. But we had to weigh that against the risk of her getting shot. The ribbons got frayed and some fell off, but we kept adding more until there were so many around her neck that only a truly horrible person would have taken aim at and shot her.

I have wonderful memories of Precious playing with my children that winter. She loved the snow as much as they did, and it was so much fun for her to chase them up and down the hills when they went sledding. She was much more sure-footed than they were in their boots and leggings, and she would leap over them and their sleds, always getting to the bottom of the hill before they did. If they fell off their sleds, she'd go back and lick them and start jumping over them again. She infuriated them with her agility.

"She's a pain in the neck!" Sammy complained. "We can't even sled with her around."

"She's rough, Mom!" Debbie summed it up. "She's not little anymore." Sometimes I'd take Precious into the house for a while so the girls could sled without interruption. They were so accustomed to living among wild animals that they wouldn't appreciate what a rare experience it was for anyone to go sledding with a deer. Perhaps someday they would treasure the memory.

While we were getting through the hunting season, we also had to cope with the mating season, and with it Precious's first heat. I noticed that she was flagging—flashing out the white area around her behind—and I tried to keep her in our springhouse during the daytime. We made a stall for her there and took her in and out a few times so she would know it was her place to sleep. We left the door open for her to come and go. But she was restless and wouldn't stay. She still came in for treats and to visit, but she was spending more time away from us.

One day when she came in I was sitting on the steps in front of our screened porch, reading a book and eating granola cookies. Precious was grazing a few feet away, and occasionally she would come over to share my cookie. We were enjoying each other's company and the sunshine when two bucks suddenly came out of the woods at the far end of the field in front of us. They were about 150 feet away.

I didn't want Precious to mate during her first heat. If she had grown up in a herd, the older does probably would have chaperoned her to keep her from breeding during her first year. But because Precious was single, so to speak, I was the only chaperone she had. And I didn't know how to be one.

The two bucks came from opposite parts of the woods and advanced slowly toward each other. Judging by the size of their racks, one was young and the other was more mature. They came toward each other until their heads almost touched; then they stood and snorted, pawing the ground with their hooves. They didn't quite touch horns. They stepped back, turned, and marched in opposite directions around the perimeter of the field. They circled back, came almost head to head again, and began to make running passes at each other. They didn't collide. They touched horns lightly, but didn't lock them. They repeated this pattern for over an hour while Precious and I watched. She was as spellbound as I was. I could see that the bucks were pushing themselves toward exhaustion, and finally the younger one went off into the woods. The other one stood there long enough for me to get a good look at him, and he was gorgeous.

He was about one hundred feet away by this time, and he began coming toward us, prancing hard and lifting that magnificent rack up into the air. There was nothing between us but a hayfield, and I could see his nostrils flaring. He was in a blind, tortured passion, blowing out of his nose and digging his hooves into the earth with each step. Precious was flashing and flirting, but staying very close to me. As the buck advanced, she ran behind me and peeked out at him.

Watching the ritual had been so hypnotic that I hadn't moved. I was still sitting on the steps. Finally I realized we had a problem. "Show's over!" I thought "This boy is headed straight for us!" He was courting Precious.

She was a little nervous. She was nudging me from behind as if she expected me to do something. I was thinking, "I don't really want to be here right now." I was looking for something I could put between us and the buck, who was still prancing stiff-legged toward us, putting his head down and lifting it up with a snort. Precious was too big for me to pick her up and take her to the springhouse, which wasn't far from where we were. I thought if I backed up into the screened porch, she might follow me inside. Then I could make some noise and try to scare the buck off. I also had to consider protecting myself in case he charged me. My father had been very concerned about Precious coming into heat and being so close to me. I could hear him saying, "You know, bucks have been known to charge women and kill them. It happens." There was a thick hedge around the porch that I hoped would prevent the buck from getting through if he decided to charge. Meanwhile he was coming closer. He was about fifty feet away.

In the midst of all my logical speculations about how

I could protect us, some other part of my brain took over. Precious was like another daughter. I got furious. I was *not* going to let that big buck get my doe. She was too young! I stood up and yelled, "Get out of here, you dumb thing! Get out of here!" I waved my arms wildly— and then *I* charged *him*! As I ran toward him, the logical part of my brain was saying, "This isn't really too clever, Jane."

The buck froze, his head high and alert. I stopped and he snorted. He was coming out of his sexual frenzy. Maybe he hadn't even realized I was there because I was sitting so still. But now I was a factor in his life. An animal's instinct to survive takes precedence over its instinct to mate. It can always get laid tomorrow as long as it doesn't die today. The buck flagged, snorted, kicked, wheeled, and ran back toward the woods.

After that experience I tried frantically to chaperone Precious. But I failed. She couldn't live free in my world, and I couldn't follow her into hers. As spring came we saw less of her, and she shared fewer of our daytime hours. She was becoming more nocturnal, which was perfectly right and natural. But I worried about her. If she didn't come in for two or three days, I was sure she'd been hit by a car, and we'd go driving around to see if there were any dead deer in the road. I was also afraid she might have dragged herself off into a field and died after being hit. Then she'd show up, eat a cookie, and vanish again. Releasing her was so hard. I didn't know how the system was supposed to work, because I didn't have a system. Precious was giving it to me a little at a time, but I didn't understand the rules yet or know what the next step was. There were many anxious moments, many heart-stopping days.

Finally I had to let go: it was the only thing I could do. I had done all I could to protect her. I couldn't do any more. When she stayed away for several days at a time, I began to get used to it. I didn't even look for her. I assumed she was all right.

We knew she had joined a herd of deer. We used to see them in the fields almost every day, and sometimes Precious would break out of the herd and come to us. Once she was grown, we couldn't distinguish her from other does except by her behavior—deer don't normally leave a herd and walk up to people. We knew it was Precious, and all we had to do was call her by name and she'd come closer. The rest of the herd stayed apart. They'd wait and stamp their feet and snort until she went back to them, but none of them ever came to us.

One morning in late spring, I was out in a field behind the house when I saw a doe and two fawns coming toward me. I stood very still so I wouldn't alarm them. The fawns were about two weeks old, old enough to follow their mother. Then the doe did something very unusual. She saw me, yet she brought her fawns halfway across the field and let them graze just a little distance from where I stood. It had to be Precious! A wild doe doesn't bring babies that close to a human being.

"Oh, Precious! Oh, Precious!" I said. "Oh, they're beautiful! Oh, Precious!" I was so touched by the loveliness of what I saw that I cried.

I didn't move toward them and they didn't come any closer, but they stayed long enough for me to look at them carefully. I had no doubt that it was Precious come to show me her babies—two tiny, delicate, cream-spotted, honey-colored fawns, all eyes, ears, and legs. Then she took them away and didn't come back. She had become wild enough to sense that human beings are a threat, yet she remembered enough of her association with me to let me know she was doing well in her natural environment. It was the biggest thank you she could possibly give me. In spite of all the mistakes I had made, because she was my first fawn and I had so much to learn, she was telling me that she had survived, reproduced, and was all right. I hoped she would live for several more years.

*   *   *

We've had many fawns at The Aark since Precious was here, and now we know how to take care of them. Precious taught us. We give them their freedom from the very beginning. We know where they go and we know they're okay. We don't keep them as close to us as we kept her. We don't handle them as much, because it isn't necessary. And we don't bring them into the house as if they were pets. Precious didn't really want to be a pet, and she communicated that information to me by staying away for longer and longer periods of time. She came in when she was hungry or when she wanted to play. Over the years I have found that to be consistent behavior, not only with deer, but with all our wild things. Once they're grown, they don't want to be bothered with people. So when we fill in for their natural parents, we let them come and go.

Occasionally a deer we've raised and released will come out of nowhere. For some reason, it happens most often when we're painting. I don't know why that fascinates them, but when we're painting and going up and down a ladder, the deer are always at the bottom of the ladder. They'll grab our shoelaces, and sometimes we almost break our necks. Then we'll turn around to talk to them—and they're gone. We've learned that if we let them come and go as fawns, they don't stay tame, and that increases their chances for survival. Every day we can see them resisting us just a little bit more. It's a very gentle way for them and us to let go of each other.

At night there's always a danger from predators—but it would be the same for fawns if they were with their mothers. Life is full of danger. Anytime I turn an animal loose, there's a danger it will fall prey to the food chain. But every time my children left the house to go to work or school, there was a danger they wouldn't come home. That doesn't mean I should have stopped them from leaving. When fawns are very young and tiny, we bring them into the barn at night. They usually come in for their bottle around sundown, and we scoop them up.

Sometimes they'll follow us into the barn as we're putting our ducks, geese, and chickens away, and there's a
lot of movement in that direction. If the fawns don't
show up, they don't go in. I let them tell me when
they're ready to stay out on their own.

When we have newborn fawns, we keep them in the
nursery for a few days, but as soon as they want to
follow us outside, we let them out for good. We don't
walk with them. We're ready with a bottle when they
come in, and then off they go again. We still try to gather
them up when a storm is coming. They know it before
we do. They can feel the change in the barometer and
they start to get edgy. All we have to do when the storm
breaks is stand outside and they'll come charging toward
us, bleating. We grab them up, put them in the barn,
and stay with them until they quiet down.

When some of our fawns are still on the bottle, they'll
be adopted by a wild doe when they start to leave. Perhaps the doe lost her own baby and the timing was just
right for her to adopt a new one. This works out very
well. If the doe isn't lactating, the fawn will come back
to us for its bottle as long as it needs one. Occasionally
it will bring its new mother along, but she won't come
in to us. She'll stand back, snorting and puffing protec-
tively, as if to say, "Don't you touch this baby." As soon
as the fawn goes back to her, she'll lick our scent off it.
After a few more visits the mother usually trusts us
enough to graze nearby until the fawn has all it can
drink. In times of drought, when our two creeks dry up,
the does will come in for the water we put out for them.
By the end of the summer, they'll come quite close to
us. We've become friends.

When I look back at the way I cared for Precious, I
shake my head over my mistakes. But I really don't know
any other way to learn. And, because I was so close to
her, I got a peek inside the world of the deer, and I'll
never forget it. I don't get that now because I don't handle our fawns as much. But I have never been able to

look at them without feeling blessed by the sight. In the morning, for instance, I may be looking out my window and I'll see a deer head pop out of the hedgerow. Then I'll see another, and another, and I catch my breath in wonder. I must have raised hundreds of baby deer by now, and I get to put my hands on them often, yet I'm always thrilled by them. When I'm driving and I see them in a field, I have to stop and watch them. They're beautiful.

8 / Coexistence Isn't Always Peaceful

Not all of my animals are wild. I've lived with dogs and cats all my life, and when you drive up to The Aark you're likely to see my two standard poodles mingling with barnyard ducks, geese, and chickens. They even play with our fawns. You won't see my cats because I keep them indoors. My cats do *not* mingle well with our birds, although they manage to get along with an occasional baby deer or fox running loose in the nursery.

Several people have warned me that it's not a good idea to let my dogs play with our fawns. "You're setting the fawns up for all kinds of danger by letting your dogs near them," one woman said. "What's going to happen when you release them and they come across some other dog?"

I thought about that for a moment, and then I said, "That's true, but I don't know how I can stop it. Besides, there aren't any strange dogs running loose around here." Then I realized that there were. Occasionally people who brought us a bird or an animal had dogs in their cars, and sometimes the dogs got out. But our fawns knew the difference between my dogs and strangers, and the minute they saw one that didn't belong, they were gone. They also knew the difference between our people and strangers. I decided not to change anything.

My house animals have had to learn how to co-exist with my wild animals because I won't give up my work with the wild ones, and I refuse to live without my pets. From the time they're puppies and kittens, my pets are accustomed to being close to wild animals. I'm too busy to keep them separated, so I put all animals, mine and Mother Nature's, in the same pens, according to their level of development. Puppies and kittens are in with baby 'coons, opossums, skunks, and anything else that fits in. If they're trashcan puppies and kittens someone has rescued, they go in with nursing wild babies.

To put it simply, I like animals. I like training them, working with them, and seeing them achieve their full potential. For wild animals, that means helping them to live free; for house animals, it means training them to exercise their natural abilities.

I was familiar with obedience training since childhood, because my mother used to train and show our Airedales. I knew that obedience training not only brings out a dog's potential but also creates a means of communication between people and their dogs. I just never got around to it with my dogs—until I had Bubba. That was a long time ago.

His registered name was Je T'Adore and he was a Bouvier de Flandres, a monstrously big, powerful dog. He was my best buddy. From the time he was a puppy, we lived in an old farmhouse with lots of land around it, and Bubba got along fine because there wasn't anyone else around. When Bubba was about four years old, we moved to a house in a suburban neighborhood, and for the first time in his life he came up against something called *neighbors*. He was the kind of dog that thought he owned everything, so he was always in our neighbors' yards—and was not very obliging when they told him to get out. I started walking him on a lead, but one day he saw a man walking down our street and didn't approve. He pulled me off my feet and dragged me halfway down the block on my face before he stopped. It became obvious to me that if I wanted to keep my dog, I had to do something about his attitude. My vet suggested taking him to obedience school, and I enrolled us in an adult education class at our local high school.

I enjoyed the training and worked hard at it. Bubba and I became very good, very fast. I took my daughters to classes with me because training is more effective if it's a family affair. Then I got interested in showing him. Training a dog for show takes a lot of time, and I don't know where I found the hours to do it, but I like competition and didn't mind the work.

Bubba was with me before the days of The Aark, but I always had several wild animals to look after, so going to shows was a challenge. I had to take my nursing babies with me wherever I went, and dogs were the only animals allowed on the show grounds. Oh, well—I had no choice but to break a few rules. I put my patients' cages on the floor of my old station wagon, put Bubba in back and Debbie in front next to me, and off we'd go. Once we arrived at the show grounds, the pace was hectic. Debbie was about ten, and a big help. I could leave her with the babies while I took Bubba to a show ring; then I'd dash back and feed the little ones, huddling down on the floor with them, before I raced to the next ring.

Bubba got his Companion Dog ribbon and learned how to be a good neighbor. Then I got a black standard poodle and took both of them to shows. The poodle's name was Muffy, and she was a ham. She had to have an audience or she wouldn't perform, so I used to pay Debbie and Leah a nickel to clap for her when we practiced. Otherwise Muffy would ignore me. At shows she behaved like royalty. She wouldn't sit on the ground; she sat on a chair.

Showing two dogs was often a matter of split-second timing. Sometimes I had to show them back to back in different rings and barely was able to hand Debbie one lead and grab the other. We managed to feed our wild animals on schedule, but in between feedings Debbie sometimes came to the rings with me so she could hold one dog while I showed the other.

In hot weather, tents were set up for large and dark dogs because they are more likely to suffer from the heat of the sun. One day the four of us—Debbie, Bubba, Muffy, and I—were taking a break under one of the tents while we were waiting for our call to a ring. We found two folding chairs, one for Debbie and one for Muffy. Bubba was comfortable on the ground, the way dogs are supposed to be, and I stood. The chairs were the old-fashioned kind, with two bars across the back and a pretty big open space between the bars and seat. Muffy couldn't get comfortable in hers and kept scooting around. Finally she scooted too far and her rear end went through the space in the back of the chair. Dog and chair went over backward. We were sitting near a corner of the tent, and Muffy somehow pulled a tent peg loose as she got back on her feet. I looked up and saw the entire corner of the tent coming down on us, as if in slow motion.

It wasn't the kind of accident that was going to hurt anybody, but it could have been very embarrassing. Before anyone noticed that the tent was coming down, I grabbed Muffy's lead. "Muffy, come!" I commanded, and she was only too happy to obey. I think she was mortified.

"Debbie, take Bubba," I said.

Walking only a little faster than usual, we made our exit. As we did, the whole corner of the tent began to waft toward the ground. As dogs and people hurried out from under the canvas, barking and shouting, some of them must have wondered how a woman, a little girl, and two dogs could be so intent on getting to a ring that they didn't even stop to look and ask, "What happened?"

At one time I had a Chesapeake Bay retriever named Zack, a grumpy, lovable dog who appointed himself my guardian and protector, whether I liked it or not. Zack had a bone disease as a pup, and until he was two years old we couldn't exercise him much. Then we had to begin exercising him a lot to build up his muscle tone. His health was a constant worry for me, and that can bring a person and an animal very close. Zack was always with me, and since he didn't particularly care for other people, he could be disagreeable if anyone else wanted to be with me. If I was sick, my kids couldn't approach my bed unless I put Zack on a down command. I used to tell them, "There's something you have to understand. As much as you all love Zack and respect him, if anything happens to me, you'll have to shoot him. If I'm in an accident and that dog is nearby, you'll have to shoot him to get to me."

The girls knew Zack only tolerated them, but they adored him. A lot of people did. Some of my friends who were into metaphysics insisted there was a spirit trapped inside of him, trying to get out. "There's somebody in that dog," they'd say. "Something's different about him." One of my friends refused to get undressed when he was in the room with her. "That dog isn't really a dog," she said.

Zack wasn't crazy about our wild animals, but he tolerated them, too. He knew he had to, if he wanted to be around me. But he left no doubt that he was in charge.

Unfortunately, when Zack was a few years old, he had a little competition in that area. It came from a turkey a man had brought me when it was a baby gobbler. The man couldn't keep it and asked me if I would take it. "Sure," I said. "I've always wanted a turkey." It was a domestic turkey, not a wild one, so there was no point in releasing him—he didn't belong in the wild. He needed exactly what we had, a barnyard.

We called him O'Rourke, which was the name of the man who had brought him. He lived free here. He walked wherever he pleased, and he slept in the barn at night. He was like my chickens—a permanent resident— and he grew to be an enormous bird. He weighed about fifty pounds at the age of two. He was as protective of me as Zack was, and whenever I went outside where O'Rourke could stand guard over me, he and Zack did their best to intimidate each other. Zack would growl and O'Rourke would gobble.

O'Rourke had apparently decided that I was his hen and was very disagreeable to any man who came near me. It was embarrassing to see him express his displeasure by taking short steps sideways and shivering his wings ferociously. Then he'd jump at the man and try to nail him with the spurs on his feet. Zack, at least, had better manners, but then, he was an indoor animal and knew a little bit about sociability. I counted on him to tolerate the turkey. I truly believe he did his best, but eventually he was pushed too far.

It was a hot, sunny summer afternoon, and a rare thing happened: I had a few minutes to myself before the next feeding. I grabbed a towel and lay down on the grass to sunbathe. Zack, of course, was by my side, but O'Rourke came following after us. Zack lay down, but O'Rourke began fussing around us.

I was lying face down, with my eyes closed, when I heard Zack growl. Well, Zack growled a lot, so I didn't look up. Then I felt O'Rourke's huge wing rest lightly across my back. I laughed. I thought he was trying to shield me from the sun. Zack definitely didn't think it was funny. His growl got deeper.

Suddenly O'Rourke climbed on top of me and settled into the small of my back like a hen sheltering its brood. He spread his wings out until they covered me completely. He had never seen me lie down, and maybe he thought I was sick. Zack, being a house animal, knew that human beings had to rest, but whenever I did he went into his *I'll guard her! I'll die for her!* mode. O'Rourke was gobbling fiercely in his *I'll take care of her!* mode.

I could see I wasn't going to get any rest. I tried to move, but I couldn't. Fifty pounds of bird on the middle of my back was more than I could throw off. O'Rourke's feet were beginning to dig into me, and I could hear that Zack was getting very upset. *I* was a little upset. But O'Rourke refused to budge.

Their confrontation happened on top of me, and so fast that I didn't see what happened. Lying face down, I had to go by sounds. I heard an awful thud and the weight on my back was gone. I got up and saw O'Rourke lying on the ground with Zack standing over him. O'Rourke was alive, but he couldn't get up.

I put Zack in the house and went back to O'Rourke. I couldn't find any wounds on him, and I didn't know how to help him because I didn't know what was wrong with him. I guessed that Zack might have grabbed him by the head and thrown him down, and there may have been internal damage. Whatever it was, O'Rourke was too far gone to save. He was dying.

I stayed with him out in the hot sun, torn between my anger at Zack and my sorrow at losing O'Rourke. Yet both of them had done what was natural to them; I couldn't blame either one of them for what happened. O'Rourke lived for about two more hours.

I was crying over his body when a bell went off in my head. It was time for the next feeding, and I was the only person around. The girls would be coming home from school, and I had to tell them about O'Rourke. As I walked toward the house, I tried to get my tears under control, but I was also thinking, "Omigosh, what am I going to do with his body?" He was such a big turkey. I didn't do anything about it that night. There was too much grief in our house.

The next morning, after the girls went to school, I

started digging a hole for O'Rourke. There was no time to waste because flies were coming in on the carcass, but as soon as I put the shovel into the earth I began to cry. I wanted to bury him next to the horse pasture because that was the softest dirt, but I needed a *big* hole. I had tears all over my face, my nose was running, and I seemed to be getting nowhere.

Those were the days when we had Billy Horse and he came over to see what I was doing. I was digging very close to the fence, and he kept putting his head over it to nudge my back and blow on me. He meant it as affection, but I couldn't receive it that way at the time. "Get out of here, Billy, get out!" I shouted at him, but he stayed.

I think every rock in Bucks County was in that dirt. As I dug them up, I threw them to one side, and eventually they formed a sizable mound. When I thought I had dug down deep enough, I went to get O'Rourke. I brought a big construction-type wheelbarrow with me, but when I tried to lift O'Rourke into it, I couldn't do it. I lifted feed bags and bales of hay every day, but O'Rourke was more than a matter of weight. It was the way a turkey, especially such a large turkey, is built that defeated me. Every time I tried to pick him up, his legs and wings slipped out of my arms. I couldn't get a grip on him.

I decided to turn the wheelbarrow on its side and roll O'Rourke into it. Then I thought, "Suppose someone drives in and sees me rolling my friend around in the dirt, trying to put him in a wheelbarrow?" The situation was gross, ludicrous. One minute I was laughing at myself, and the next minute I'd burst into tears, remembering something wonderful O'Rourke had done. Finally I got him into the wheelbarrow, but he was upside down and his legs were sticking out. When I wheeled him back to the horse pasture, Billy Horse was there, waiting for me. But horses are afraid of dead things, and he took one look at O'Rourke and ran off, screaming.

I was wet from sweat and tears, but I was trying to give a little dignity to the occasion by easing O'Rourke down into the hole from the wheelbarrow. But the shape of the bird was so awkward that he flopped out, his legs and wings aiming in all directions. That's when I saw that the hole was too shallow. I pulled and tugged at him, trying to get him into a better position, but I couldn't move him. I was crying again and could hardly see through my tears as I tried to fold and stuff his wings and legs close to his body. But as soon as I let go of a leg it would pop out and up.

Whenever one of our birds and animals dies, I always thank God for the blessing of its presence in our lives, and I ask him to receive its little spirit—it's big spirit in O'Rourke's case—into His kingdom. I should have been getting ready for his entrance prayer, and there I was, holding his leg down with my foot. I took my foot away and his leg popped up, sticking straight out. I was exhausted. I was getting ticked off. So I did a quickie prayer. "Okay, God," I said, "take this guy, 'cause I'm losing it." Then I started to cry. I couldn't just leave him there like that. He was my friend. He had been my protector. Now I had to protect him.

Then I saw the mound of stones. In some ancient cultures stones were a proper grave cover. Why not use them for O'Rourke?

It took me the rest of the afternoon to build a pyramid of stones over the too-shallow grave, but there were enough of them to keep anything from digging him out. O'Rourke was decently entombed, and the stones were a fitting memorial. You can still see them if you pass that way. I often do. It's a lovely place to spend a little time, remembering.

9 / "Mary Jane'll Get You If You Don't Watch Out!"

Nineteen eighty-nine was the coldest December on record in the Philadelphia area. I remember it very clearly because a few volunteers and I spent a lot of hours in an unheated warehouse trying to trap a recalcitrant red-tailed hawk.

The warehouse was owned by the City of Philadelphia and was located on the docks along the Delaware River. It hadn't been used very much lately. In fact, the second story was sealed off and hadn't been used at all for years, except by pigeons. They got in through broken windows and made their homes inside. Then an inspector cited the city for violations, namely the pigeons and the dirt they produced. A cleaning crew was called in to evict the pigeons, and that's when they discovered that a red-tailed hawk had also taken up residence on the second floor. Since the hawk was protected by federal law, the cleaning contractor called a Philadelphia conservation officer, who in turn called a rehabber in the Philadelphia area. The rehabber didn't have a permit to handle birds of prey, but she knew that I did. So she called me.

It was a few days before Christmas. Usually that's a slow time at The Aark, and I was planning to throw myself into baking and decorating for the holidays. My whole family was going to be here on Christmas Day: Debbie and her husband, Ricky; their daughters—my granddaughters—Rebecca and Nicolina; Leah and her fiancé, Vince; Sammy. It was a rare opportunity for me to bask in the pleasure of having them around me.

But—a red-tailed hawk in a warehouse? I couldn't say no, although I had never tried to trap one in such circumstances. "Sure," I said. "Give me the address."

Philadelphia, although not so many miles from Newtown, is light years away from us in terms of congestion. And I wasn't thrilled about going down to the docks. It wasn't where you would expect to find a hawk. How did it get there? How long had it been there? Fortunately, I was more intrigued than scared.

I have worked with many different birds of prey, and from some remarkable falconers I've learned a great deal about how to handle them. When I have a problem I don't hesitate to call for advice.

"My God! The docks?" my falconer friend said when I told him what I wanted to do. "They eat little girls like you for lunch down there! Are you going alone?"

"No," I assured him. "I couldn't possibly carry all my gear alone." Then I asked him what kind of trap he recommended, and he offered to lend me a Swedish goshawk trap. It was a big, clumsy, two-tiered cage, with a sealed compartment on the bottom for bait. The bait was to be live pigeons, but they wouldn't be sacrificed because the hawk couldn't get to them. Ideally, the bird would fly down into a large compartment on top of the pigeons and the opening would close.

I couldn't fit the trap in my Bronco, so I borrowed a truck. I took my assistant director, Maia Neeley, with me. Maia is young and attractive, but you couldn't tell by looking at her because she had taken my advice and bundled up beyond recognition. The two of us looked like walking cocoons with eyes. Maia was excited. "How long do you think it'll take to get it?" she asked me.

"A couple of hours," I said. I tried to conceal my apprehension about going down to the docks. I had been all right until the falconer made his comment. Then my mother expressed her concern. Then my father said, "The docks are no place for a woman!" I don't think he had ever been there, but, like many people in less populated areas, he had visions of terrible things happening to women in that part of the city. And his fears were getting to me.

Once we arrived, however, the dockworkers were as nice as they could be. This was something different for them. They helped us carry our gear into the warehouse and wanted to know how we planned to catch the hawk.

I had been told that the warehouse was the size of three football fields. To me, it seemed bigger. It was two stories high, completely enclosed, with thirty-foot ceilings. The only way to get to the second floor was by two staircases, one at each end of the building. The light was dim and we had to get used to it. The first thing we saw was the ceiling, a spiderweb of I-beams that supported the massive structure. The second thing we saw was the hawk. It was a mature, handsome red-tailed hawk, with a body about eighteen inches long and a forty-eight-inch wing span. Its chest was a light cream color, the feathers on its wings were dark brown, and its tail was red. It wasn't flying below the I-beams, but flying right through them! It was breathtaking to see it maneuver in and out of them without clipping its wings. Since there is no way to determine the sex of a red-tail short of surgery, we couldn't tell whether it was a male or a female. But it sure looked healthy. And no wonder. Red-tails eat pigeons, and this one had been inside a building full of them. It was living on Easy Street! No wonder it hadn't tried to leave.

"It all depends on how hungry it is," I said to Maia. A hawk can easily go for ten days without food. If there's a bad storm or severe temperatures for days and days, it'll sit quietly so it doesn't burn up energy.

As the hawk flew over us, I could see that its crop was full. Someone had told us there was one pigeon left in the building. Well, not anymore. And from the way the hawk maneuvered among the I-beams, I was sure it had lived there for some time.

"This could take more than hours," I thought. "This could take days."

As our eyes grew accustomed to the light, we could see that the second floor was almost empty. There were some broken file cabinets in one area and old desks in another. One corner was piled high with cardboard file boxes, and there were a few large, empty wooden boxes, the kind used to load cargo on ships. It seemed to be a warehouse for rubbish. There were windows all around, but some were painted over and the rest were dark with soot. That accounted for the dingy light. The broken windowpanes had been closed up with something opaque to keep the pigeons from coming back. They also kept the hawk from getting out. If we couldn't get it, it would starve.

The building wasn't heated and hadn't been for years. It jutted out over the river, which was frozen. The cold was damp and numbing and the air was stale and dirty with city soot. Sounds were strange, too. They echoed. We had brought some hot tea in a thermos and we shared a little before we set up the trap. We used a few pigeons from The Aark as bait. They were totally lame and would have been euthanized because they couldn't fly. I should have put them down, but I didn't. But they would be safe in the goshawk trap.

For four hours Maia and I sat inside one of the cargo boxes, not saying a word, and blowing vapor out of our mouths and nostrils. We couldn't even move around to keep warm. Meanwhile the hawk soared and perched, soared and perched, always above us, never anywhere near the trap. Finally I said, "It's not even interested. It's got a full belly. Let's go home." We gathered up the trap and carried it down to the truck. It took us a long time because we both were stiff from sitting motionless in the cold. Everything we wore was filthy with soot. When I got home I undressed in front of the washing machine and tossed everything into it. Then I climbed in a hot tub. I didn't think I would ever feel warm again.

The next day I took Diane Nickerson with me. I brought a different kind of a trap, but it made no difference. For four more hours we sat in a cargo box and the hawk stayed up among the I-beams. A few times, in the midst of absolute silence, we were startled to hear footsteps echoing from all parts of the building. They turned out to be dockworkers coming up to see how we were doing. By then I was getting to know some of them by name.

"Did you get it yet?" Joe would ask.

"No, Joe, not yet," I'd whisper.

"When do you figure you will?" Sam wanted to know.

"Can't tell. Soon, I hope."

Occasionally men came upstairs, one at a time, carrying file boxes. They'd put them down and leave. Since we were hiding from the hawk inside our big box, they probably didn't know anyone was there, and I debated whether or not to make our presence known. It was an eerie experience, because we were so vulnerable. We could be murdered up there, and nobody would find our bodies until they began to stink—and that wouldn't happen until spring because it was so cold. I decided it was better for everyone to know we were there, so the next time a man came upstairs I got out of our box and introduced myself. I asked him please to go downstairs as soon as possible so he wouldn't interfere with our job. I did the same thing when other men came up, and most of them were very understanding. Some waited around for us downstairs so they could ask questions.

When we left that day I told the cleaning contractor we wouldn't be back for six days. "That hawk's got to be hungry by then," I told Diane.

Waiting allowed me to be home for Christmas, but I didn't have time to prepare for it. I decorated our tree hastily on Christmas Eve and spent the evening at Debbie's. On Christmas Day I had everyone at my house, but there were no cookies, no breakfast cakes, no special touches. My mind was on the hawk.

I was trying to figure out how it got into the building. It was obvious that the pigeons got in through the broken windowpanes, but they were small panes and large birds like red-tailed hawks usually don't fly through small openings. This one must have flown in on the thrust of a kill. It was probably going after a pigeon and suddenly found itself in the wrong spot. But it had all it wanted to eat as long as the pigeons were there. Since hawks don't drink much, the pigeons also supplied all the fluid it needed.

The building had such low doors and high ceilings that when the cleanup crew tried to drive the hawk outside, it simply flew high and never came down to the level of the doors. Besides, the light outside was much brighter than it was inside, and that in itself would have kept the hawk from going through an open door.

Maia, Diane, and I went back to the warehouse a few days after Christmas. We took still another kind of trap, but the hawk ignored it. I had been on the phone to every falconer I knew, asking for advice, but so far nothing worked. How much hungrier did the hawk have to get?

On New Year's Eve day it's hard to get anyone to do anything except celebrate. But I was able to gather up four people: Diane, Maia, David, and David's son, Aaron. I had made up my mind that this was the day we were going to get the hawk. Two of my crew had other commitments, so we set a time limit for ourselves. We would try another trap for two hours, and if we couldn't get the hawk, we would run it down. The hawk *had* to be hungry, and that gave us an advantage.

For two hours we shivered in our boxes while the hawk lighted on beams more than it flew. "Time!" I called, looking at my watch and climbing out of the box. We would have to run the hawk down, which meant we would chase it from perch to perch until it was sufficiently exhausted for us to catch it. This was a last-ditch effort, and would be very hard on us and the bird.

The five of us stood in the middle of the enormous floor, devising our strategy. We divided the second floor into five sections, one for each of us—four of equal size and a strip at the end. I took the section on the end, which ran straight across the building but was relatively free of the debris that cluttered the other four sections. By then the hawk was so flighty that all we had to do was run toward it; it wouldn't light.

At first the hawk stayed in my section, which meant I was running back and forth the length of a football field. When I reassigned us, posting two of us at the end, the hawk started flying out of that area.

After an hour of racing around that sooty floor in subzero temperatures, it was a question of who would wear out first, the hawk or us. Not only were we running at a furious pace, but we were shouting directions, and still we could barely hear each other. Our lungs ached and we were limping from shin splints. Even Aaron, the youngest of our crew, was coughing. The area was so vast that we could hardly recognize the people at the other end as people.

Finally the hawk started panting and seemed to miscalculate. It tried to land on a beam, missed, and started to go back up to the beam. I knew it couldn't stay up there much longer. It had to come down.

It did. It landed on a pile of boxes and just couldn't summon the energy to fly again. I ran in with my long-handled net and threw it over the bird with one swoop of my hand. I wore a heavy falconer's glove on my free hand and reached over the hawk's shoulder, grabbing its feet and gathering its body to me. It couldn't open its wings and hurt itself, and it couldn't open its feet and hurt me.

The crew gave a hoarse cheer, and we all sank down on the dusty floor. The hawk was panting heavily and was obviously dehydrated from all its exertions. There wasn't time to take it back to The Aark for treatment; the bird needed help right then and there. I couldn't be sure its dehydration was life-threatening, but it definitely was health-threatening, and this had been a very healthy bird.

I started pulling my spittle up because that was the most available source of fluid. I dribbled some into the hawk's beak, and it drank readily. I had to bend my head close to its beak, which alarmed Aaron. "You're going to get bitten!" he warned.

"I'm okay," I told him. I wasn't worried about the bird's beak because hawks don't use their beaks to defend themselves. They use their feet, and their talons are strong and sharp. A hawk's beak is designed for tearing meat and it's used for eating. Make no mistake about it, though: if a hawk bites you, you're going to miss some part of yourself. I've been bitten on my face by some, and they've taken a good hunk, but usually they were hawks that had been handled by human beings, and, like wild mammals kept as pets, they behave unpredictably. This hawk, however, was too exhausted to foot me or bite.

As it drank my saliva, it began to revive. "Okay, everybody, get your spit up, *now!*" I said, because I was running dry. We all took turns, and as the hawk regained some energy, we increased the distance between our mouths and its beak. Then we all ran dry, and we resorted to the tea in our thermoses. It was too messy to pour the liquid from the thermoses into the hawk, and most of it missed the beak, so we took some in our mouths first and dribbled it into the bird. When it was strong enough for us to move it, we took it down to the truck and headed for home. I continued dribbling tea into it, and by the time we were halfway to The Aark, the hawk was on its feet and close to fully recovered. I had a chance to examine it carefully and it was feather-perfect. I was right: it had never bumped into those I-beams.

I kept it with us overnight, just to be sure it was able to go off on its own. I put it in a four-by-four pen and gave it a good meal. It ate every bit and drank plenty of water. The next morning I let it out of the pen. It perched in one of the big trees for a few minutes, and then—zoom!—it was gone.

It took two days for our lungs to stop hurting from all the soot we had inhaled running the hawk down, and we had such severe shin splints that we could hardly walk. But watching that hawk fly out far and away was a beautiful sight. It made up for all the aches and pains.

Usually, when birds of prey are brought in to us, they aren't in such good condition. Very often they've been hit by a car because they were down on a road hunting rodents. At night, when temperatures drop, the roads stay warm, and the heat attracts rodents and small animals. That's when so many of them get hit by cars. And the bird of prey that comes in to pick up a rodent often gets hit by another car. Owls get hit at night because that's when they hunt. Hawks hunt in the daytime, but they can get hit, too, if they're after a rodent on the road.

If a hawk or an owl is brought in with a broken wing, which is a common injury, we tape the wing to the bird's body. Years ago we used to pin the wing, using a metal pin to secure it, but sometimes that made the wing stiff and although the bird recovered, it couldn't fly. Taping is a much better procedure, but it's important to use paper-backed tape because it doesn't damage the bird's feathers. Birds can't fly well if their feathers are crushed or lost, so we take measures to protect them. Unfortunately people often bring us birds with wings already taped with regular adhesive tape. By the time we get the tape off, the feathers are in sorry shape and that's a problem in itself. Some people think they're helping the bird by removing adhesive tape with chemicals, but at the same time they also remove the natural oils from the feathers, and that hinders flight.

When an injured raptor, or bird of prey, comes in, the first thing we do is put the bird in a container that doesn't allow it enough room even to try to open its wings. For a few days it may have to be hand-fed. This is our version of intensive care. Once the bird is able to feed itself and can stand comfortably, we put a low perch into the container. This allows the bird to get up off the floor and protect its feathers. Without a perch, the bird's tail feathers will rest on the floor and get bent and crushed and full of fecal matter. As soon as possible after the bird can perch, we move it to a four-by-four pen, where it has more space and a bigger, thicker perch. I use logs rather than dowels for perches because they're rough and bumpy, and that keeps the bird's feet clean and healthy. In this way we can prevent the bird from developing foot problems while we're working on the problems it had when it came in.

My four-by-four cages are solid on two sides and screened on two sides. For raptors we use dowels instead of screening on two sides. We keep the birds quiet and in semi-darkness while they're recuperating. We also paper-tape the bird's wings to its body to keep them from hitting the sides of the cage. Once the bird is doing well, we move the cage outside where it's lighter, but not too bright.

When we take the tape off the bird's wings, we move it into a flight pen, which is eight feet high, fifty feet long and twenty-five feet wide. One quarter of the roof is enclosed, and the rest is covered with close-set dowels and wire screening. Plywood runs halfway up each side; the rest is made of dowels and screening. The bird has enough space to fly inside the pen and gets plenty of light and air, but it doesn't have to feel threatened by a dog or a 'coon or a person walking by.

We put several perches in the flight pens, at different heights, so we can begin to exercise the bird. We run at it to make it fly from one perch to another. When it begins to pant, we stop, because that means the bird is tired.

The time in the flight pen varies with each bird. The healing of a broken wing usually takes about three weeks with the wing taped, and another week or two bringing the bird up to full flight. Some don't need much of a workup before they regain their flight; others need more. It depends on the injury and the age of the bird. When we release an adult bird, it usually leaves like a bat out of hell and we never see it again. If it's an immature bird or a youngster that didn't have flight before its injury, it will usually hang around and come in for the food we put out for it.

I release a bird of prey after it's flying well in its pen. I take it out to the middle of a field where I can watch it for a long distance to see if it has a strong, even flight and can lift itself up. If it can't lift, I've got plenty of room to go out and retrieve it.

When we release a bird of prey, we don't assume that it will be able to feed itself right away. It may need time to get back into the hunting pattern, or, in the case of young birds, to learn how to do it. So, after we release a bird, we follow a falconry procedure called "hackout." It's similar to what we do when we release mammals. We put food out for it and gradually reduce the amount, depending upon how much the bird comes in and takes. We put the food up on top of the flight pen or on a pole or a flat area where the bird can come in and take it. We put out the bird's normal amount of food for four days; then we cut that amount in half for three days. We allow it to get a little hungry——not to the point where its health is threatened, but enough to awaken its instinct to go after something on its own. Then we go back to the normal amount again. Hackout is a substitute for the mother bird feeding her young, teaching them to catch food, and finally encouraging them to catch on their own. When the bird begins to leave some food, we know it's caught something. Instinctively it will take a large live mouse over a pile of fresh food. We subtract what's left from the normal amount and that becomes the new normal. When the bird leaves a lot of food, the leftover amount becomes the new normal. This is how we push the birds out without endangering them.

I remember a great horned owl that had been hit by a car and was brought in with a broken wing. We fixed it, released it, and about two months later it came back. It had unusual markings so it was easy to identify, and it sat in a tree over the barn for about four days with its feathers ruffed up, which was like saying, "I'm sick." It wouldn't come close enough for us to touch it, so we put antibiotics in some food and put it on the roof of the barn where the owl could get at it. Given my choice I would have used a bigger dose of antibiotics for a longer period of time, but to do that I would have had to trap the bird, and I didn't think it was a good idea to add to its stress. For a couple of days the owl ate everything we offered it, and then it disappeared. But while it was here, we could see it getting better each day.

Because we release so many birds and animals throughout the year, we almost always have some hackout going on. We keep track of the birds by watching for repeat visits. If we stand out under the hackboard, nothing happens, but as soon as we back away, the birds come in. Then it's easy to see who's coming in and who isn't.

The hackout process allows me to free my patients more quickly because it lets them decide when they're ready to let go of me. It takes some birds longer to let go because they've had medical problems that necessitated my handling them and they begin to trust me. That's a lovely experience, but I want them to get over it for their own well-being, so I release them as soon as they're physically recovered. I put food out for them for as long as they want it. At The Aark, where I don't have people living close to me, I can let a bird take its time. I don't have to worry about a bird of prey landing on a neighbor's head and causing a commotion.

Birds of prey are meat-eaters, and feeding them while they're at The Aark takes some ingenuity. A few years ago I would have said they eat meat and nothing else, but I was wrong. I had a little kestrel in a cage with vines growing on the sides, and I let them grow to give the bird shelter from the sun and weather while it was out-doors. The kestrel ate all the leaves it could reach, which told me that birds of prey must take in some greens. Think about it—when a hawk eats a rabbit, it also eats the grasses in the rabbit's stomach. When a peregrine falcon eats a dove, it also eats the grain in the dove's crop. But if we were to give our birds of prey grasses or grains as food, they'd perish before they ate them because they don't recognize them as food.

While our patients are here we feed them every day, but hawks and owls have one no-feed day a week. A screech owl eats a medium-sized mouse a day when he's in captivity and not burning up a lot of calories; a great horned owl eats five mice a day, and a youngster will eat ten when it's still growing and producing feathers.

We buy cockerels from a hatchery, but sometimes we don't even get a chance to freeze them because we have so many birds of prey. We also buy quail from hatcheries that raise them for falconers and for human consump-tion, but they're expensive. They cost a dollar a bird, and a great horned owl will eat at least two per meal.

Birds of prey need a balanced diet. For instance, if we offered them only cockerels, they would get too much vitamin A. Out in the wild they eat all kinds of things, sometimes whatever they can get, and we try to approxi-mate their natural diet. Sometimes, at the end of a semes-ter, schools offer me mice and rats that have been used in behavior-study programs, and I'm glad to get them—but only if they're dead. These are clean mice and rats; they haven't been exposed to chemicals, so I don't have to be concerned about poisoning my patients. I won't accept them alive because I don't want to be the one to kill them, and I also don't think it's prudent to feed my patients live animals. Something live will try to get away, and a recuperating bird might get hurt trying to catch it. There are people who give their raptors stunned mice, but I think that's inhumane.

Frankly, one of my best sources of food for birds of prey is roadkill. Almost every day my volunteers and I go out looking for animals that have been killed on the road, which my license allows me to do. We have to be very careful about what we pick up. We don't go into rural areas because hunters go there and an animal that's dead on the road may have been shot. We don't want to feed our birds of prey something that's full of lead because it will poison the bird. We don't use any roadkill at all for eagles because even the slightest amount of lead can be fatal, but for hawks and other raptors we try to be selective. We go into residential areas where hunting is prohibited, and we look for animals that are fairly intact.

Many of my volunteers are a little squeamish when I ask them to bring in any good-looking roadkill they see on their way to The Aark. But in no time at all they get over it. Each morning almost every one comes in holding up a dead squirrel or a rabbit as if it's the greatest gift in the world. To me, it is. I put it in a lock-top bag, pop it in the freezer, and know that it's going to be just what some patient needs to get it eating again.

I must admit that occasionally I still feel a bit awkward about stopping my car on the road and getting out to pick up a dead animal that, to many people, is a sight they can't bear. Sometimes I can do it without stopping my car. I slow down, open my door, and grab—but it takes practice and most people don't have occasion to develop the skill.

When I began seeing Donald Stretch, who later became my husband, he learned very quickly that if he showed up at my house with flowers in one hand and a road-killed squirrel in the other, the squirrel made a better impression. It's not that I don't like flowers—I do!—but the squirrel is life-sustaining.

I put Donald to the test quite early in our relationship. We were on our way to Philadelphia for dinner and the ballet, which Donald knew I adored. It was still light when we left The Aark, and as we were winding along the roads leading to the highway that would take us directly to the city, I spotted something in the road. "Stop!" I said. "It's a rabbit! A good one!"

Donald pulled over and stopped, completely bewildered. At this point he had seen many of my patients and knew a great deal about my work. What he didn't know was the source of my food supply for birds of prey. He thought he was coming to a rabbit's rescue.

"No," I explained. "It's a dead rabbit. It probably got hit by a car—but it's in good condition."

Donald looked at me as if to say, "So?"

"I need it," I said, opening my door and getting out. "What I mean is, my raptors need it. Wait here."

Usually, when I do these things, I'm wearing sweatsuits and sneakers. Not that evening. I was in my dressy best, high heels and all—*not* what you'd expect to see walking along the shoulder toward a small, dead, furry body. When I got closer I saw that the rabbit had been badly damaged. My raptors couldn't use it.

Donald had been sitting patiently, and when I returned to the car he said nothing. I liked that. He seemed to realize that I must have known what I was doing, and that if I felt like telling him about it I would. And I did. But before I could finish describing the feeding habits of birds of prey, I saw another rabbit on the road ahead of us. Donald avoided hitting it and pulled over to the shoulder without even asking me if I wanted to stop. Once again I got out and high-heeled back to where the rabbit lay. This one must have been struck in the head; otherwise it was intact. I reached down, picked it up carefully and started back to the car, holding the body out in front of me to avoid getting my dress dirty. I was so excited about the find that I forgot about the rest of the world. Cars were passing swiftly, but I didn't notice them until one came along with a little boy half hanging out the window. "Mom! Mom! Mom!" he shouted, pointing at me as he passed. The car slowed down for a moment, then sped away.

In the wild world, where human beings haven't taken over, dead things are recycled. When one creature dies, another creature eats it. If there weren't animals to eat dead animals, we'd all be overcome with corpses and disease. Recycling is part of the ecosystem, and it's very effective.

It's even a shame to bury a dead bird. Its soul is gone, so why bury it? How much better to put the bird in a back corner of a yard and let the opossums get it. In that way, the dead becomes a gift to the living. If we can't stand to see dead animals and birds on the road, we can take the time—and summon the fortitude—to stop the car, get out, and move the creatures off the road so the crow, opossum, or vulture can get to them without becoming another casualty. At the same time we'll be removing dead animals from the path of people who like to run over them—and there are plenty of those.

At The Aark, we have many patients that don't survive, and when they die, we recycle some of them. When birds fly into our windows and die, they go right into a lock-top bag and our freezer, because when we get a sharp-shinned hawk in, birds are all it will eat. We have to pay attention to the natural diet of our patients, and sometimes that turns out to be former patients. In fact, the saying around here among my family and volunteers is: "Don't sit real still, 'cause Mary Jane'll get you!" My kids used to tease each other when they got sick: "Don't sit around on the couch too long or Mom will cut you up and feed you to the owls." To some people recycling may seem unappetizing, but it's better than getting run over. I see it as nature's way of accepting death and respecting life.

The longer The Aark is here, and the more people become aware of the threats to wildlife, the more patients they bring us—and the more opportunities we have to educate the public. The level of social consciousness about the environment is rising, and even if people don't know we exist, they get involved with wild things because they realize how important it is. Then they call the police, a veterinarian, a nature center, or an SPCA, and that's how they find us. Very often people who bring us animals for the first time will say, "Oh, God, I'm so glad to know you're here! You can't know what I went through to find help." A few years ago those same people might not have noticed a wild animal in distress. Now they do. They want to do something, and if they don't know how to help, they seek out someone who does. This is why our practice increases each year.

Once people know we're here, they become even more aware of wildlife and they get involved more quickly. It's not a dramatic situation anymore; it's normal. The first time people bring something in, it's usually a bigger animal because it's more obvious to them and they relate to it as if it were a human baby. But when people realize that help is available, they become more observant of all wild things and they're less hesitant to get involved with something smaller, such as a featherless baby bird. At one time they might have walked away from such a tiny thing, if they even saw it, because they didn't know anything could be done for it. Now they bring it in to us or call us to ask what they can do to help.

Some will even bring in a vulture, which is not your

most lovable bird. One day a woman called and said there was a strange-looking bird under her porch. "Please, help us," she implored. "I think it's sick, but we can't get near it. It's enormous!"

When she described the bird's ugly head and feathers, I knew it was a vulture. I decided against telling the woman how to get the bird, because a vulture can give you an awful bite—I lost part of my lip to one, and I'm a professional! And, when all else fails, a vulture will throw up on you. That's one of their weapons of defense and it's very effective. When a vulture is down on a carcass, it gorges itself, but then it has to stay on the ground for a while because it's too heavy to fly. It needs air movement to get a lift. If anything tries to get at it while it's in such a vulnerable situation, it throws up and, believe me, it's awful! It's not as foul-smelling as skunk spray, but it's usually enough to make you throw up, too.

I sent Maia to get the bird, and when she brought it back I could see that it was very sick. It had been poisoned, which is unusual for a vulture because its digestive system can tolerate almost anything. It probably ate carrion—a rat, perhaps—that had poison in it. A lot of wild things are poisoned by some of the chemicals we use on our lawns. Then they die and they're eaten by predators and birds of prey. Something like that must have happened to the vulture. Fortunately someone noticed the bird before the poison had been in its body for very long and we were able to save it. We gave it a shot of atripine, and by the next day we were able to release it. But who knows how many more poisoned birds of prey die out there in the wild where nobody sees them?

If an injured bird recovers, but can't fly anymore, we don't always put it down. Sometimes we can use it in our educational programs. We do many programs for schools and civic organizations, and we always include live animals. Now we're beginning to do some programs here at The Aark. Nothing gets the attention of people more quickly than a live animal, and it's the best way to help a child fall in love with our planet. Seeing a live hawk, an eagle, a bunny, or a bluejay allows a child to connect with other forms of life that share its world. It's better than anything on film. We start lecturing to a bunch of kids and show them some wild animals, and we get crapped on—it brings the house down! Or we get bitten, and the kids love it! The animals are real. They're unpredictable. And they get the message across.

If I kept every bird that couldn't be released, I'd have no room for anything else. I won't sacrifice a good cage for a bird that can't go free. I want the perfect cages for the birds that can be released. But if I can't use a non-releasable bird for educational purposes, other people can. Nature centers, academies of natural sciences, and zoos offer educational programs several times a day, and they use live animals. They don't go out and trap them; they get non-releasables from rehabbers. There are organizations throughout the country that keep lists of available non-releasable animals and match them up with lists of animals other people need. We often get calls from organizations looking for a particular bird or animal, and if we have one, we're only too happy to send it along because if we accumulate too many non-releasables, we have to destroy some of them.

I used a beautiful red-tailed hawk in my educational programs for almost three years. I don't know whether it was a male or a female, but it was a great favorite with children. Originally the bird was brought in with a broken wing, probably from a car hit since it was found along a road. The wing healed but was slightly out of whack, and the bird couldn't seem to get good flight. I kept it in a flight pen for a long time because it *almost* flew the way a hawk should, and I was hoping time would make the difference. But it didn't. The bird managed to get up on the high perches, but when I tried to flush it to make it fly, it flew down instead of up. Some birds fly around the pen so well that I just open the door and they go. But not this one. I decided to put it in our educational programs.

Schoolchildren got to know the hawk and would ask for it. It was good on the fist, which means it was trained to sit on my hand while I carried it, turned it around, and lifted it up. It could turn its head all the way to the back, which delighted the kids. I could get it to fan its tail so they could see how a hawk looks in flight, and it would talk to me so they could hear its voice.

One day I was in the hawk's flight pen, raking the dirt and cleaning up, and as usual the bird was on a perch. Usually I'm very careful about doors, but apparently I hadn't closed the pen door firmly, or perhaps it swung open—and the red-tail flew straight over my head and out. It was a wonderful experience to watch it climb. I was thrilled!

The first thing I did was load the hackboard with food. I knew the bird wouldn't go far because, after three years, The Aark was its territory. Then I saw it in a tree. When I stepped back, it came down for the food and went back up to the tree. It did that for days, but I could see that it was acclimating itself to the wild. It took some time for it to regain its flight strength, but when I last saw it, it was flying as well as a hawk should.

I learned something from that experience. Now I'm very cautious about sending non-releasables to organizations that use them for educational purposes. If a bird's wing has been amputated, then there's no chance it will fly. But if a bird has both wings, we'll keep it for a year or more, just in case we underestimated its chances to fly. Once they're in an educational situation, people look at birds in a different way. They may not have a place to hack them out if they suddenly regain their flight. Or they may not have enough space to test their ability to fly and stay up. Furthermore, people handle them so much that the birds don't even make any effort to fly.

I thought I had given up on that red-tailed hawk, but

maybe not. When I saw it fly out of its pen, something deep inside me seemed to nod and say, "Yes!" I think it was a little flicker of hope that may have been there all along.

I O / The Great Egg Scramble

Hatching eggs is a tricky business, even for the birds that lay them. When human beings try to hatch them, they rarely succeed. The procedure has to be done very carefully or the results can be disastrous. If the humidity isn't properly maintained, if the heat isn't exactly right, and if the eggs aren't turned often enough, the baby birds can be deformed—if the eggs hatch at all. That's one of the reasons why I don't like to hatch eggs and try to avoid it. The other reason is that there are enough orphaned birds in this world without our hatching more.

Some people take offense at my attitude. They come across a nest of eggs with no mother in sight, so they bring the eggs to us because we have incubators. If they're the eggs of an endangered species or a species that's just beginning to come back, I'll take them and do what I can. Years ago, I hatched quail eggs to repopulate the species in our area. I also hatched bluebird eggs as part of a Pennsylvania Game Commission project in a state park near The Aark. I've hatched many owl eggs because the owl population is down. But mallard eggs, Canada goose eggs, and many other overpopulating birds' eggs—no. It's better if we don't.

I tried to explain my reasons to a young family who brought in three mallard eggs they found when their dog chased the mother off the nest. When the mother duck didn't return, the husband and wife decided to hatch the eggs themselves. They thought it would be a wonderful lesson in natural science for their little boy, and all they wanted from me were instructions. I tried to talk them out of it. I told them that if they went ahead, I wouldn't help them.

"We have more mallards than the habitat can feed," I told them.

"But there are new creatures inside these eggs," the woman said. "Don't you want to save them?"

"To me they're not alive until they hatch," I said. "Besides, there's a good chance the eggs aren't even fertile."

I explained that not all eggs are fertile. Even in the same nest, some eggs aren't fertile and they won't hatch. And since the mallard mother didn't come back—unless she was killed—there was good reason to suspect that the nest had already gone wrong.

My other concern about neophytes hatching eggs is that when the babies reach the point where they should begin to acquire the behavior of their parent species, they don't. Instead, the babies begin to follow the human beings around and they don't learn normal behavior. We call it "imprinting," and we see a lot of imprinted birds and animals at The Aark. Sometimes we can undo it, but even if we can it takes us a very long time.

For some reason which I have never been able to figure out, the eggs we do want to hatch are inevitably the ones that are hardest to rescue. Occasionally we have to take a few risks. For instance, many years ago, shortly after I came to the farm in Newtown, I received a distress call from the Mercer Museum in Doylestown. This is a wonderful old establishment where prized hand-crafted tiles have been made and exhibited for generations. The building looks like a reproduction of an old castle where knights and ladies and court magicians dwelled. Its high walls are made of concrete, and its terra cotta roof is turreted with openings originally intended to house pigeons. But barn owls had moved in instead.

It was Eastertime and the weather had been unseasonably hot. In one of the openings where a barn owl had laid its eggs, the high temperature was hatching the eggs ahead of schedule and the babies were trying to escape the heat.

"I know you'll find this hard to believe," the man on the phone told me, "but the little owls are jumping out of the nest onto the ledge below the opening. One of them landed on its head and died. We just don't know what to do! Is it safe to go near them?"

The museum was about fifteen miles away. "Don't go near them," I said. "Put something soft on the ledge so they won't hurt themselves if they fall. I'll be right there."

Tom Fitzpatrick was helping out in the nursery, and I asked him to come along. I knew I would have to use a ladder to get from the ledge to the opening in the turret, and I wanted someone steady to hold it.

When we arrived at the museum, two members of the staff pointed to the opening, which was a good two stories above the ground. One more bird had fallen out, but it landed on the blankets the staff had put down. Tom and I took a ladder with us and went up on the ledge. One of the staff members went with us. We found the fallen owlet and it seemed to be all right. We had brought along a box lined with soft towels, and Tom put the bird in it.

As I climbed up the ladder to the turret, I caught the familiar, rather disgusting smell of an owl's nest. When owls make their kill, they eat bones, feathers, and all, and regurgitate it as something called castings. Then they eat the castings, feeding bits and pieces to their young. The combination of castings and fecal matter gives the nest its telltale odor—not exactly the kind of thing you want to inhale on a hot day. Whenever I attempted to get owl eggs out of a silo, I could at least count on some ventilation in the structure, but the museum was solid concrete, which not only heated the air in the turret but trapped it as well.

I couldn't see into the opening because it was dark in there, so I reached in as far as I could and felt around. "Tom, I just might have to come down in a hurry," I called to him. "If Mama Owl is in here, I'm in trouble!" If she was, and if she nailed me, I might go right off the ladder. Tom and a staff member braced my legs against the ladder so that if I fell back suddenly, I wouldn't go off the ledge.

I could feel five newly hatched babies in a nest, but no Mama Owl. I pulled the owlets out, one at a time, and gave them to Tom to put in the box. Then I reached in again just to be sure I hadn't missed one. I felt an egg and thought, "Oh, it's probably a dud." I was going to leave it there, but then I felt movement in it. My fingers also detected a crack in the shell. As I was bringing it out, I perhaps put too much pressure on it and the egg began to hatch in my hand. I felt the shell give and as I brought my hand out I saw a tiny owl in it. The little rascal turned right around and started to foot me! Its behind and one leg still in the shell, it was trying to sink its talons into me! It was 100 percent owl!

We were able to save every bird in that clutch, even the one that had fallen onto the blanket, and eventually we returned them to the wild. But we really couldn't claim credit for hatching Mama Owl's eggs. That belonged to the weather.

I have my husband Donald to thank for making it possible for me to rescue some other owl eggs in a rather unorthodox manner. We literally flew out to get them.

Donald and I had been seeing each other for over a year, and there were times when my commitment to my work got in the way of our relationship. But Donald was equally committed to his business, a company, started by his father, which manufactured fabrics used in airplane interiors. He worked long hours and got involved in every detail. The difficulty, as Donald used to put it, was this: "I don't understand how anyone can give her whole life over to something that doesn't earn a lot of money." My response was: "I don't see why I should let my patients, who are completely dependent on me, be inconvenienced—or even suffer—when a fully grown adult can take care of himself."

Neither Donald nor I is comfortable in confrontations, so these expressions were as close as we came to an argument when something I had to do interfered with something we both wanted to do together. Gradually, though, we were discovering that our feelings for each other went very deep, deep enough to make it possible for us to accept what we didn't quite understand in each other. What we did understand, and what we admired, was far more important, and we were beginning to talk about the possibility of marriage. We weren't in a hurry. We agreed it would take a lot of thought. Donald had three teen-aged children from a marriage that had ended in divorce. I had been divorced, too, and had three children, although two of mine were out of their teens. My daughter Debbie was married and a mother. Leah was living on her own, and only Sammy was home with me.

A less important, but frequently bothersome difference between Donald and me was our attitude toward flying. For most couples, that would hardly be a problem; but it was for us because Donald had his own plane and looked for any excuse to fly it. He had to use it for business and loved using it for pleasure. I could make peace with flying in a large commercial air liner, but I was terrified in a small private plane! Donald had already taken me up in his plane several times, insisting that I would get over my fear, and it wasn't happening. Instead I sat rigid, from takeoff to landing.

Then, one day, I received a call from a couple in Lancaster County who had discovered a nest of owl eggs when part of their silo caved in. They were farmers and had a lot of respect for owls because they keep the rodent population down. "The parents got killed in the cave-in," the man told me, "but the eggs are okay. I think they could be saved."

The problem was time. With the parent birds gone, the eggs needed to be placed in an incubator as soon as possible to maintain the heat they required to hatch. But Lancaster County was quite a long distance away. Then I had an idea. "Is there any place on your farm where a plane could land?" I asked the man. "A small plane."

"We've had planes land here before," he said.

"You mean you have a landing strip?"

"I wouldn't call it that," he said. "It's an area where a plane can land. It's all grass, mind you."

"That might be okay," I said. "I'll call you back in a few minutes."

I dialed Donald's office number and he was in. When I told him about the owl eggs, he listened patiently, but when I asked him if he could possibly fly me out to get them, I knew I had his attention. "Good God!" he said gleefully. "What a decadent reason to fly a plane—owl eggs!"

"It would take too long to get them by car," I explained. "A plane is the only way."

"Do you realize it will cost me about—let's see, with gas and time—about one hundred and sixty dollars to get your damned eggs?"

"Donald, will you or won't you fly me out there?"

"You know, Jane, this is one of the problems I have with you," he said, only half-teasing. "You're so damned determined. I have the feeling that if I don't say yes, you'll find some other way to get those eggs."

"Donald, I repeat, will you or won't you fly me out there?"

He sighed. "You know I will. No problem. I just wanted to be a hero, I guess."

"I don't need a hero. I need a first-class pilot and that's why I called you."

He was all business. "Okay, it'll be getting dark when we leave and dark when we get there. Call your farmer and get me some navigational information so I can find his place."

I called the farmer and got what Donald needed. "We'll have some lights on for you," the man said. I foolishly forgot we would be landing on farmland and envisioned instead the landing lights along an airport runway at night.

I met Donald at the Mercer County Airport, where he kept his plane, a single-engine Piper Cherokee 6, and we took off for Lancaster County. Usually Donald was totally relaxed in his plane and I was tied up in knots, but for some reason I wasn't nervous on that trip. Owls need all the help they can get. All I could think about were those owl eggs and the possibility of saving them. When we reached the area where the farm was, it was too dark for us to see it, but Donald was going by the navigational information the farmer had given me. "We're in the right place," he said. "It should be directly below us. He did say they had lights, didn't he?"

I nodded. I was looking down into inky-black emptiness, realizing for the first time that when there isn't any light, there isn't any depth. In other words, you can't tell whether you're an inch or a mile above ground. For a second, my old panic returned and I realized I was in a small plane, but then I thought, "Relax—Donald knows what he's doing. Don't be a pain in the ass!"

"Look!" I said, pointing to a tiny flicker of light below. "Is that a light?"

"If it isn't, it'll have to do," Donald said, and I felt the plane descending.

We saw a few other lights, tiny ones. Later we learned that they were from flashlights held by the farmer and his neighbors. They had also opened the barn door to let the light shine out for us. They meant well, but their improvisation was a far cry from the lights a pilot needs to land at night. Oh, well, we had landing lights on the plane. They would help.

It was probably the most beautiful landing I will ever experience in a small plane—because I was totally ignorant in my bliss. All I had on my mind were owl eggs and what we could do for them once I got them back to The Aark. I did not know what Donald suddenly realized as we began to descend: we had no landing lights on the plane. That afternoon, while he was working on the plane's engine, he had removed the cowling and disconnected the landing lights. When he put the cowling back, he forgot to reconnect the lights, so when he switched them on, nothing happened. He had nothing but the light from inside the barn and a few flashlights to guide him in. There was nothing to warn him of obstructions, such as trees or other outbuildings, and nothing to give him any sense of how close the earth was to our plane as we came down toward it.

I sat back, waiting for the familiar bump-BUMP! of the wheels touching the ground, and it didn't come. I did notice Donald's hands on the control wheel, and his knuckles were white. I had never seen them like that before. Then, mercifully, came a clunk-CLUNK! as the wheels hit the ground, and I assumed the difference in the sound came from landing on a grassy field instead of a landing strip.

Only later did Donald tell me his side of our adventure. While I was in the barn getting the eggs, he removed the engine cowling and reconnected the landing lights. Then he paced off the grassy strip to be sure it was long enough for our takeoff.

I had told the couple how to use a heating pad and a wet towel to keep the temperature and humidity up without getting the eggs wet, because that would have done a lot of harm, and they had done a very good job. I carefully packed the eggs in a basket lined with hot water bottles. The couple and their neighbors came out to the plane with me and waved their flashlights at us as we took of. We couldn't help feeling a little bit heroic.

As we flew home, I held the basket on my lap, ready to cushion it against any turbulence we might encounter. When I'm in a small plane, the very mention of the word "turbulence" is usually enough to make my hair stand on end, but that night I felt invincible. I still didn't know about the missing landing lights. Donald told me after we landed, when my feet were on firm ground.

"No wonder your knuckles were white!" I said. "Why didn't you tell me?"

"And spoil the best ride you ever had?" he said. "Besides, you were so calm, you kept *me* steady."

Donald got quite involved with those eggs. He helped me put them in an incubator and wanted to know how it worked. Every day, whether we spoke on the phone or he came out to my house, he wanted to know what was going on. "Are they hatching yet?" he would ask.

"No."

"Let me know as soon as they do," he said. "As soon as the first crack—okay?"

"Okay," I promised. I was enjoying his interest. It was the first time he really got involved with my work, but he did it in a way I appreciated. He didn't become an overnight expert. He didn't make silly suggestions. He just let me know that he thought what I did was important. I only wish that he could have been in on a success story, but unfortunately it wasn't to turn out that way. The eggs didn't hatch. I didn't know why. Perhaps, even by flying out to get them, we had allowed too much time to elapse. Perhaps there was something about the flight back that wasn't good for the eggs. Or perhaps we human beings simply aren't adept enough at hatching eggs.

Finally I had to tell Donald. I called him before he could call me to ask about the eggs. I could feel as well as hear his disappointment. "Oh, gee," he said. "Oh, hell, that's—" He was silent. So was I.

That evening, when I was doing the seven o'clock

feeding, I looked up and there was Donald, standing in the door to the nursery, filling it up the way he always did. I remembered being startled at his size the first time I saw him. But his boyish face, with its well-trimmed beard and intelligent blue eyes, gave him the look of a gentle giant. "Hi," he said. "I was just passing by—having gone about twenty miles out of my way to do it—"

I was holding a tiny stomach tube in the mouth of a baby opossum, so I kept my hand steady and nodded.

"You look tired," he said.

"So do you."

"Can you use some help?"

"Tonight—yes. That would be great."

He came in and looked down at the little wild thing in my hands. "You'll have to show me how," he said.

"Sure. It's easy. It just takes some patience."

As he pulled up a chair and sat down, holding his hands out for the opossum, he frowned. "I have to make something clear," he said. "I don't want to do this all the time."

I put the animal into his hand and waited for him to grasp the tube. "I don't want you to do this all the time, either."

"What I'd like to do is clean up your grounds. They could use some attention—and I enjoy that sort of thing."

"I'd like that."

For a few minutes I held my hands over his until I could feel him getting comfortable with the animal. Then I let go. Donald was doing fine. Just fine. We both were.

II / The Truth Is, I Love Bats!

I did everything wrong with my first bat. I broke all the rules I had followed for years, ignored everything I had learned about wildlife. I fell in love to such a degree that I was beyond reason. I took the animal into my home and my life, and in trying to save it, ended up killing it.

The bat was brought in by a man who found it on the floor of his living room. "I just opened my closet door to get my jacket, and it fell out," he said.

"Maybe it fell down from the attic through a crack in the closet," I said. That could have happened easily. It was a hairless little baby, only about an inch and a quarter long, and emaciated. It was so tiny I had to use a magnifying glass to find its mouth so I wouldn't accidentally give it milk through its nose. An eyedropper was much too big; so was a doll's bottle. I used a syringe, replacing the needle with a thin white tube that's almost as narrow as a needle but blunt on the end.

This happened only a few years ago. In all my time as a rehabber, I had never had a bat for a patient. One reason may be that most people don't want to be bothered fussing over a bat. Often they're afraid of them because so many myths have grown up around them.

But once you understand what a bat is, you can't help but love them. At least, I can't.

Bats are not rodents; nor are they birds. Bats are mammals, the only flying mammals in North America. They're incredibly valuable because they eat insects: one bat can catch up to six hundred mosquitoes an hour. They aren't at all interested in people. If a bat comes near you, it's because there's a bug near you and the bat wants to get it.

I was excited about my first bat because it was an opportunity to learn about the species. But the more I learned, the more I loved them all. They're so beautiful. They have two feet and two wings, and what we call wings are actually velvety, fur-covered skin that extends from foot to foot on each side of their body. Underneath the fur and the skin are long, thin bones, like fingers, that enable the bat to fly and scoop up bugs.

The little baby took the milk I offered it and fell asleep. It was a little brown bat, which is fairly common in our area, and eventually it would have soft brown fur all over its body. It looked so helpless and weak that I was afraid to leave it. I stayed in the nursery most of the night, and whenever the bat awoke, which was about every two hours, I gave it more milk. That was as much as I could do for it, because I didn't know enough about the behavior of bats to understand what a baby needed. I didn't even know what to feed it once it was off milk.

The foremost authority on bats is a man named Merlin Tuttle, president of Bat Conservation International and a brilliant scientist who conducts educational programs all over the world. I decided that if anyone could give me reliable information about the little guy in my nursery, it was Dr. Tuttle. I telephoned him at his office in Austin, Texas, and he was very generous with his advice.

"What kind of life would this baby have if it were living with its mother?" I asked him.

He told me that bat mothers protect their young beneath their wings even when they're flying; the babies hook themselves onto the mother's fur with their feet, the way baby monkeys cling to their mothers. A bat mother usually has one baby at a time, and, being a mammal, she nurses it. When it gets too big for her to carry and it's almost ready to fly, she transfers it to a nursery. It would hang upside down, by its feet, from a ledge or a rock it could grasp. When bats begin to fly, they have to drop down and then swoop up. That's their normal flight pattern, but they must have that drop before they can come up. This is a critical time for bat babies. If they let go of the ceiling and drop but don't swoop up, it's Good-bye, Charlie!—because even if they live through the fall, their movement on the ground is so slow that they are easy prey for ground-dwellers.

After Dr. Tuttle explained this process to me, I looked at the little bat in its cage and thought, "Oh, well, I've done sillier things than try to be a bat mother." I removed it from its cage and placed it upside down on my sweatshirt. Sure enough, it dug its little claws into the fabric and seemed perfectly content.

"What's that on your shirt?" Donald asked when he came home that evening.

"It's the bat," I said. I told him about my conversation with Merlin Tuttle.

"How long will this have to go on?" he said.

"I don't know. It's my first bat."

"Next thing you know, you'll be giving it a name."

"I did. His name is Bruce."

"Let me guess—Bruce Wayne? Batman?"

"Naturally."

"Jane, you don't approve of naming your patients," he reminded me.

"Well, this is different," I said in my most authoritative tone. After all, I wasn't going to tell him I was losing my head over a bat. "I know what I'm doing." And I did. I knew I was doing something wrong.

For the next few weeks Bruce—I was actually calling him Brucie—was always with me. I hung him on my clothes and took him everywhere with me. Donald went along with it, but I could see he wasn't happy sharing me with a bat. He also was concerned that I was losing too much sleep. For thirty days I fed Bruce around the clock at two- and three-hour intervals. Sometimes during the day I'd get a four-hour break, but he was particularly hungry at night, so I was hardly sleeping. I was developing a typical bunny-hugger's attitude that I was the only person in the universe who could care for this animal, and I refused to let anyone else take over his feedings. I was so exhausted at one point that I couldn't speak coherently. Finally even I realized that I had to let Bruce go.

Following Merlin Tuttle's advice, I had weaned him from milk by starting him on mealy worms and then insects. He was a handsome animal with soft brown fur, but he wasn't even attempting to fly, and that worried me. "Mom, he eats like a pig and you feed him too much," Debbie had the courage to tell me. "Look at him—he's too fat!"

She was right. Bruce was a roly-poly bat. I vowed to put him on a diet, but I never did. Instead I started hanging him on a curtain in the nursery at night. I put a mover's quilt on the floor so he'd have a soft landing if he let go and dropped. He adjusted very well. Sometime during the night he must have dropped down, but he didn't swoop up, because every morning when I went down to the nursery, there he was, scuttling across the floor toward me, his wings flopping at his sides. I was certain that one of those nights he was going to succeed, and when that happened, I would release him.

Every summer Donald goes to the Midwest on business and I go with him. Before we left that year I told everyone—staff, volunteers, and family—to be sure to put Bruce's landing strip down at night. We were away for ten days, and when we came back Bruce was dead. Someone forgot to put the quilt down. During the night Bruce must have dropped down, didn't swoop up, and landed on his head.

I was heartbroken, but I blamed myself, no one else. I did the very thing I accuse so many other people of doing: I killed an animal with misguided kindness and love. Bruce couldn't fly because he was too fat, and I made him that way. I loved feeding him. I loved wearing him, playing with him, and having him with me all the time. I didn't allow him to be what he was: a bat.

Since Bruce I've had several bats, and although I play with them more than I should, I don't try to turn them into pets. Most of our patients are small brown bats, like Bruce, but sometimes we get red bats, which have long, bright red fur. We once had a mother red bat with two babies on her, and, thanks to Merlin Tuttle, I knew what to do. I left the babies on her, and when she was well enough to leave she took them with her. We released her by putting her on the underside of a big leaf, and while we watched she flew off.

Some experts believe that when a baby bat has been hand-raised, it can't be released successfully. But I've heard similar misgivings from people who say you can't release a hand-raised deer or a 'coon because they'll always come back, and I haven't found that to be true. Releasing bats that come in to us as adults is no problem, but we've had only one experience releasing a bat that came in as a baby, and I'm not sure how successful we were.

I had been on my best rehabber behavior with that bat. I didn't overfeed it or fuss over it. When it began to flutter its wings a lot, I thought it might be ready to fly, so I watched it closely. One night I had done the late feeding in the nursery, and when I looked at the bat, I said to myself, "This baby is ready!"

I was so afraid it might crash-land that I took it up to our bedroom where it could hang on the framework of the bed and drop onto something soft. Donald had gone upstairs earlier, and he was asleep when I brought the bat in. I stood on the bed and reached up to hang the bat from the framework, being careful to move gently. I thought the bat was hanging onto the framework, and I let go. The bat let go at the same time and fell down onto the pillow, defecating as it went. Donald woke up. "Oh, my God!" he said when he saw me standing over him.

"Don't move your head!" I warned him.

"Why not?" he said.

"There's a bat on one side and a mess on the other."

He didn't even move his eyes as I reached down and scooped up the bat.

"Jane?" Donald said, still a bit groggy. "What's going on?"

"I thought the bat was ready to fly!"

Good sport that he is, Donald finally got into the spirit of the event and cheered the bat on as I made two more attempts to hang it over the bed. But it didn't fly. The next night we tried again, and it flew across the bedroom and crash-landed on the rug. Fortunately it wasn't hurt. I decided to move the action outdoors.

For four nights we went out at twilight. Donald stood on a ladder and held the bat as high as he could and let it drop. I stood waiting to catch it in case it couldn't achieve flight. "Don't you think maybe this time the experts are right?" Donald said. I was thinking the same thing—almost.

On the fifth night, Donald dropped the bat, and the little thing came straight down and then swooped up in a big arc. It got very excited and started chasing bugs, darting back and forth, up and down, just the way a bat should fly. "Hey! Go for it!" Donald shouted, and I started cheering. He came down off the ladder and lifted me off the ground with a gigantic hug.

"Wait a minute! Wait a minute!" I said, getting my breath. "Where's the bat now? I don't see it."

"It's too dark—that's why," Donald said.

We searched the area thoroughly with our flashlights in case the bat was lying on the ground, but we couldn't find it. That's why I can't be certain we succeeded in releasing a hand-raised bat. But for the next several nights, when Donald and I went out at twilight just to take a look around, we did see a small bat out there hunting. Of course, we couldn't prove scientifically that it was our bat, but we like to think it probably was.

12 / The Power Goes Out, the World Goes Away

When we have a power failure at The Aark, it's more than an inconvenience. It's an emergency, because lives are at stake. There is no "right moment" for power failures, and there isn't much we can do about them. If they last a long time, we go outside and talk to God—real loud.

If it happens in the daytime, the first thing we notice is the immediate silence. We live among so many electrically powered devices that we don't hear them humming until they stop. It happens in an instant. The incubators, isolettes, freezers, fans, the air conditioners in the summer, the heating system in the winter, the well, the lights—nothing works. At night we run for candles and flashlights.

My first concern is for the babies in the isolettes. The humid warmth our machines provide substitutes for that of the wild mother, and without it the babies can't survive. We combine them, crowding more bodies into fewer units, and we keep them tightly closed so the animals can generate their own heat. If that isn't sufficient, we grab the animals and stuff them in our shirts, putting our own warm bodies to good use. I can't tell you how many bras and T-shirts have been filled with little squirrels and rabbits! If the power failure goes on for more than a few hours, we know we'll lose some babies, usually those that are in critical condition. That's hard to take, yet sometimes I think it's God's way of telling us we're just not meant to save them all.

My next concern is for water, because our well operates on electricity and we need water as much as we need isolettes. We can't make the animals' food without water. We can't clean them or their cages, and that can threaten their health. So I get in touch with my neighbors to see if they have power. If they do, I can get water from them. If they don't, I buy bottled water at the supermarket—if there's any left.

I used to be able to get emergency water from a hundred-year-old hand pump on our property. No matter how long it sat unused or what the temperature was, I could always go out there and in twenty pumps I had water. Then the gasket finally went, and I thought, "This old pump has served me well and it's time to retire it." I put in a brand-new hand pump only to find that it won't work unless it's primed, and I can't prime it if I don't have water.

Down under my springhouse there's an ancient open well where I can get water that's suitable for washing but not for drinking. This is a last resort because it takes a long time to lower a bucket in just the right way to make it sink instead of float. I also have to be careful not to fall into the well because the wall around it is very low.

During a power outage, I do not want help and I try to get everybody out of the house as quickly as possible. That includes staff, volunteers, and even my husband, Donald, who does not take kindly to leaving, because he genuinely wants to help. Many people want to help, but if they don't know how, they get in my way, and at that point, I don't have time to teach them. Whatever I have, in terms of energy and knowledge, I try to save for the animals. Their lives depend on it. When other people are around, they use water and need food, and they're so dependent upon electricity that they don't function well without it. They create dirt that has to be cleaned up, and they moan and complain when we have to improvise. My daughters are the only people I can have around me, because they've gone through these emergencies with me since they were children and I don't have to tell them how to deal with them. They can function in a raw environment, which is what a power failure forces people to do. For instance, the toilets don't work, so we have to go to the bathroom in the woods. When I bring in water from the open well, I pour a little into a pan and we wash at the sink. It's like having to reduce matters in your life to camping level when you're not in the mood to camp. Try getting toothpaste out of your mouth when you don't have water. It takes three times the effort. I use a small propane stove to heat water for the babies' bottles, and I pour the water into a pan with great care because I don't want to spill a single drop.

If people come in with an animal, I explain, "I have no power," and send them home with instructions. "You can do more for it than I can right now," I tell them. They always cooperate.

I really prefer to be alone when the power goes out. I can handle it better. I can even have a little fun with it. I just turn my clock back about a hundred years to a time when people didn't have electricity and try to imagine how they would have done things. My house has been around for about 260 years and lived a long time without our modern conveniences, so I try to learn from it. I get a little peek into how women lived a hundred years ago, and I have great respect for them. Keeping a house comfortable and putting food on the table took enormous effort then. Washing dishes was a major task because water had to be carried in and boiled. Wood had to be carried in to fire the stove. In winter people had to be careful not to open their doors more than absolutely necessary because they didn't want to let the heat out. They had to think ahead about every move they made.

In a power failure I have to do the same thing. I can't take anything for granted. I have to plan what I'm going to do, or I'll create more problems for myself. I have to consider each action I'm going to take and what the reactions might be. Will it involve water? Will it result in something I have to clean up with water? How much light will I need? I have to change my routines and try to use the daylight hours to the fullest. I don't want to do something in the dark hours that requires more light than I can get from candles and flashlights. Concentrating on such simple, everyday matters makes a person very tired.

Ordinarily, when people have a power failure, their telephones work, but mine often doesn't, maybe because I have so many lines and hold buttons. We can't call out, but people can call us. We hear the phone ring, yet when we pick it up, the line is dead. And it rings constantly because, I suppose, friends are trying to get through to see how we are. After a while we wrap rags around the bell so we don't have to listen to it ring.

There's a hardness to life without modern conveniences, but there's also a softness to it that can be quite wonderful. The softness is the feeling that the world has gone away. I wouldn't want it to stay away, but it's nice to have the break from the pressures of civilization. It reduces life to its simplest needs and brings me closer to nature. I learn a little more about myself because there are fewer distractions. The lack of power slows me down. I have to stay where I am. I can't leave the farmhouse because I can't turn my responsibility over to a gadget. I'm afraid something might go wrong if I'm not here to monitor it. This is not an uncomfortable anxiety or a feeling of dread; I *want* to be here. I want to look after things. I trust myself.

Sometimes we've been isolated even when we kept our

power. Several years ago, when my daughters were in school, we were snowed in for a week. It was wonderful because we don't have many patients in winter and everything, even the heating system, was working. But we couldn't get out to the road and no one could get in because the snow was so deep. It was also very cold, so the snow didn't melt.

Getting food was difficult. The feed mill truck would come as far as it could, which was about a mile from our house, and we'd meet it with the children's sleds. We had to make more than one trip because they were small sleds and couldn't carry everything. The only way we could get our food was to walk to the stores, and they're a couple of miles away. The snow was so deep that walking was a slow, strenuous effort. Then we ran out of fuel and the oil truck couldn't get in. In those days I had an old Mercedes diesel, and I kept a tank of fuel for emergencies. We found we could use diesel fuel in our oil burner, so we made endless trips to the tank, which was quite far from the house. Eventually the township had to come in with dump trucks and backhoes to dig the snow out and haul it away.

For us, in many ways, it was a good time. The snow forced us to do everything in slow motion, and when we went to bed at night, we slept very soundly! It wasn't only that we were physically tired. We were tired mentally from planning each move we made.

The last deep snow I remember was about ten years ago. It started during the night, and when we woke up we couldn't even see the barn because the snow had drifted ten feet high and covered it completely. I switched on a lamp, just to see if we had power. We didn't.

"Okay, girls, grab a shovel!" I called. We had animals in the barn—chickens, ducks, geese, and two horses—and they had to be fed and watered. But first we had to dig our way in.

The snow was up to my waist, and it took all day to dig a path into the barn. Then we had to clean the horse stalls; no matter what happens, that has to be done every day or you're going to have sick horses. It was bitterly cold when we started, so we piled on as many layers of clothes as we could carry. I found that a long quilted skirt was warmer than pants over long underwear, so I threw fashion to the winds. I added sweaters and a down-filled coat, pulled my big boots over my heaviest socks, tied a babushka around my head, put my earmuffs over it, and stuck my hands in mittens. When I stepped outside, the girls took one look at me and fell down laughing. It was a good way to begin the day.

The horse stalls are in the back of the barn, quite a trek from the manure pile outside, and we had to make the trip at least three or four times to clean each stall. Three of us maneuvered the wheelbarrow while the fourth one stayed behind and worked in the stall. We took turns as to who did what, so we each got a break.

We had shoveled an area around the barn, but rolling a wheelbarrow over snow is never easy. Manure is heavy, so we couldn't overload the wheelbarrow, which meant we had to make more trips. We had packed the trail down as best we could, but still we kept getting stuck. I was pushing the wheelbarrow, and the girls were pulling, and we were giggling all the way. The fun got us through the work.

Mucking out a stall is hard work. You get hot. No matter how cold it is when you start, you work up a sweat and have to start taking some clothes off. You put them back on when you go out in the cold and push the wheelbarrow, but underneath your clothes, you're all wet. It's a wonder we didn't all get pneumonia.

We weren't worried about keeping the horses warm. We had put their covers on the night before—their "pajamas," we called them—and a healthy horse keeps himself warm. We let them out to play in the snow for a while, and they had a wonderful time. The chickens, ducks, and geese bundled up to each other. The barn sheltered the animals from the wind, and that's what they need. With the windows and door closed, and horses giving off a lot of heat, it's a warm, toasty place. Sometimes we'd find a thin skim of ice in the water buckets, but all the animals were fine.

Our wood-burning stove kept the first floor of our house warm. We kept it cranked high and went out for wood a couple of times a day. We cooked on it, too. When the food in our freezer began to thaw, we put it out in the snow and decided what to cook by smelling the packages. Whatever smelled the strongest was our next meal.

In those days I used to make my own bread. It took longer to bake it on a woodstove, but the smell of it made us feel as if the house were giving us a huge, warm hug when we came inside for the night. Homemade bread was more than food to us; it was a way of sharing something with special people. When our blacksmith used to come to shoe the horses, he always brought us some bread his father had made. In the winter, shoeing horses is a cold job, so the girls and I would stay out in the barn with him and talk to him while he worked. When he finished, we'd come inside to get warm, and we'd sit around the hearth eating the bread. We got to know the man very well, and he used to bring his girlfriend with him to see the animals. When they got married and had a baby, they would bring the baby—and the bread.

At night I would burn so many candles in the living room that I could read. Of course, when we went up to bed it was pitch-dark. Debbie and Leah didn't mind the dark, but Sammy did. "I'm scared," she'd say at the foot of the stairs, reaching for my hand.

Debbie and Leah, each with a candle in hand, went ahead of us. "Sammy, don't be silly," Leah said. "There's nobody up there."

"You don't know for sure," Sammy said, in her determined way. "You can't see what's up there."

"Sure, they can," I promised her. "Here, take a candle.'' I put a candle in her hand and lifted her arm, showing her how to move the circle of light ahead of her. "Watch your sisters. See how the candles open up the darkness? Now you and I can do the same thing with ours." Sammy's sense of the romantic pushed her fear aside and she let go of my hand. Walking a step ahead of me she followed her sisters up the stairs, lifting and lowering the candle, playing a game of tag with the darkness.

The heat from the woodstove didn't reach upstairs, and it was very cold, but we kept warm in the way people have done for ages: we bundled up with each other. Our cats and dogs sleep in bed with us, anyway, so they were welcome buddies. Sleep came easily as we began to snuggle in our own warmth.

We had done our chores. We had taken care of the birds, the animals, and one another. It was satisfying, knowing we had earned our rest. When the power came back on, which might happen at any moment, we would have our machines, gadgets, and conveniences again, and we would certainly appreciate their help. But with them would come the preoccupation with things that only seemed to matter. It was refreshing to know that life doesn't always have to be that way, that sometimes it's more meaningful when it has to be simple.

I used to fall asleep on those snowed-in nights comforted by the realization that outside the animals had their world, and inside we had ours. Yet we were part of each other. We depended on each other. That's the way the world is. At least, that's the way it is to me.

Epilogue

Springtime comes early to The Aark, often before the trees begin to bud. I know it's here when my phone starts ringing and doesn't stop. After the stillness of winter, I'm ready for the sudden activity. It excites me.

Long after Donald has gone to work I'm trying to eat my breakfast, which has long since cooled. Maia Neely has gone to get a Canada goose someone saw injured along a road. Diane Nickerson is out in the barn, cleaning cages and making a list of the ones that need to be repaired. I'm left to answer the phone.

Most of the calls are from last year's volunteers. They're coming out of winter's hibernation, too, and they want to know when I can use them. A few new people call to offer their help, and I tell them that my volunteer list is filling up quickly. "I can only use you if you can give me four hours at a time," I say, and that eliminates some of them. I wish I could take them all, but I don't have enough time to train them in a formal manner. "The best way for you to learn is to walk in my footsteps and watch what I do," I explain. "And you won't learn much if you come in for an hour here and another one there."

I put my plate of sausages and pancakes into the microwave for a few seconds and try again. I'm very hungry. As the phone rings again, Maia returns with the injured goose under her arm. The call is from a prospective volunteer who heard about us from a friend. "I've never worked with wildlife before," she tells me. "But I'd love to!"

Thanks to the long cord on the phone I can talk to her and examine the goose at the same time. Maia has put the bird on the kitchen table. One wing is broken at the joint and part of the bone is protruding. "Smell it," Maia says.

I bend down and sniff at the break in the wing. "Ugh-h-h!"

"I know—it's bad, isn't it?" Maia says.

"Let's give it some antibiotics. That infection may be too far gone, but we can try."

"Can we fix the wing?"

"Maybe. But the goose won't ever fly. Not with that kind of break."

Maia picks up the goose to take it to the nursery, which is now in a small building a few feet from the back of the house. Then I remember to tell her what to do with two of our patients. "Oh, Maia," I call to her, still holding the phone, "the red-tail is eating."

"Great!" she says, a happy smile coming to her face.

"He started eating a little bit of the cockerel you put out this morning. Take a look at his cage and see if he ate more."

"Okay," Maia says, opening the door. Then she hesitates. "What about the barn owl?"

"Let's see if he'll eat. I took a mouse out of the freezer about two hours ago. If it's defrosted, put it in with the owl and watch what it does. If it's starting to eat we can release it soon."

Maia nodded and left for the nursery, and I became aware of a buzzing sound coming from the phone in my hand. Oh, dear, I had forgotten about the woman who called. She must have heard our conversation and hung up. It wasn't the best way to introduce a newcomer to the joys of rehabbing. On the other hand, perhaps it wasn't so bad. One way or another, people who want to help us have to get over being squeamish.

My breakfast is cold again, but I finish it. If the phone will just be quiet for a little while, I will take a great blue heron out and try to release it. It's been with us for about a month. A man who was walking with his dog along the Delaware River found the bird. Its wing was broken and the bird was very weak because it couldn't catch fish. It was recovering well, but I had tried to release it a few times and failed. The wing appeared to have healed, but the bird just couldn't get into the air.

"We can use him in our programs," Diane suggested. She was now doing a lot of our educational work.

"If he can't fly, we will," I said. "But I'd still like to give him another chance. I'm sure that wing is okay. Maybe he just needs to be taken to the right kind of place."

Diane takes over the phone as I go to get the great blue heron. I want to take him down to a marshy place along the Churchville Reservoir, near the nature center, where I used to work. It's a perfect habitat for the bird, with tall grasses along the banks and plenty of fish in the shallow water. All the bird has to do is bend down and pick up a meal with that long, slender, powerful beak. But if it can't fly, I won't leave it there to become a prey for something else.

It's early afternoon and sunny, but the air is still chilly. The heron won't mind; it can take a certain amount of cold weather. It had obviously elected to stay in our area that winter. I'm wearing hip boots so I can walk out into the marshes, but it's a slow journey because I'm carrying the big bird in its cage. The water is shallow quite far out, and I can see fish.

I put the cage down on a small hummock of grass and open the door. "It's okay. C'mon out and take a look around," I say. "I won't leave you—you'll have to leave me."

It's a lovely heron, and the sun glistens on its blue-gray plumage as it comes out of the cage onto the wet grass. It walks off into the water and takes a few uncertain steps to one side and then the other. Suddenly it extends its large wings and lifts itself off the water as if it had never been earthbound. As I watch, it flies some distance out into the water and comes down in a perfect landing.

"Omigosh!" I'm not sure whether it came down for good or stopped to eat. I see its head dart toward the water and a glint of sunlight on a small fish caught in its beak. I wait while the bird finishes its meal and pokes around in the water. It's beginning to feel at home. A few minutes later it rises into the sky and flies off in the opposite direction until I can't see it any longer, not even with my field glasses. I can't tell you how happy I am!

When I come home, Maia has more good news. The red-tail is eating well, and the owl has eaten half its mouse. Diane is in the nursery with a woman who brought in some baby squirrels. They're so young that their eyes are closed and they have no fur.

"Who's on the phone?" I ask Diane.

She fits a nipple to a doll-sized bottle of milk. "Go see," she says, picking up one of the squirrels.

As I walk into the kitchen, I hear my granddaughter, Rebecca, Debbie's oldest daughter, speaking to a caller. "If you'll hold on, I'll go get my Gam. She just drove up, and she can help you. Please hold on." She turns and holds the phone out to me. She is very proud of herself, and well she should be. Becky is five years old and one of my most accomplished volunteers. She can feed the fledglings almost as well as I can, and she may handle the phone even better.

She gives me a hug and heads for the nursery. Knowing her, I'm sure she wants to help feed the squirrels. As she closes the door behind her, I can't help wondering if maybe—just maybe—she might someday decide to take her love for animals a little farther. She might even become a rehabber. I must confess, that's my favorite fantasy. But, after all, it's a pretty good profession.

Postscript

A lot of people want to become wildlife rehabilitators, but only a few do. The reason is simple: it's very hard to make a living at it. A salaried job is rare in this field because hardly anyone wants to spend money preserving creatures who seem to be on the way out, or a habitat that could be developed.

But it's becoming apparent that unless we all learn how to coexist with other species of life on this planet, the planet itself will cease to exist. Creation is wondrously complex. Each part of the ecosystem depends on other parts. Take a species as basic as worms. If worms don't aerate the soil, plants don't grow. If we don't have plants, we don't get oxygen. If we don't get oxygen, we can't breathe. Without worms and dirt and rocks and trees, we can't live on this planet. I'm not wise enough to understand how all of the many links in the chain of creation influence each other, but I have to believe that there must be a purpose even for the cockroach. If we break the chain, we're in trouble. We're beginning to realize that now.

Extinction is part of the ecosystem, too. And that's okay if it happens naturally. As a species becomes too large, too small, or too specialized, it no longer serves the needs of others and it begins to die out naturally. That's the way evolution works. A species isn't meant to go on forever and ever and ever. If we try to prolong its existence, it becomes a species lingering on the brink of extinction, and that's a terrible way to live. Or die. We don't need dinosaurs today. The planet doesn't need them because, over thousands of years, it has shifted and changed.

When a species goes down naturally, usually there are one or two other species coming up from the bottom to take its place. The key word here is *naturally*.

Evolution makes sense when it happens *naturally*. When man gets into the act, things can go disastrously wrong. Today man is hastening the evolution process so much that there isn't time for other species to fill the gaps left by those that are wiped out before their time. Too many species have already been wantonly eliminated. But even more ominous is the elimination of the habitat that supports so many other living things. The extravagant use of pesticides and herbicides by farmers and homeowners is wiping out the food supply of our birds and wild animals. It is deforming their offspring before they are born. Only now, because this same poisonous practice is threatening the water we drink, are we becoming aware of how much damage we've done. Only now are we beginning to see that survival may mean something as simple as sharing our world with ants and mice and dandelions.

My hope is that wildlife rehabilitation can help man slow down his hastening to extinction. If we can learn how to rebuild the kind of habitat that will allow species to go on repopulating naturally, then maybe we can repair some breaks in the ecosystem's chain. And maybe we all can hope to hang around a little longer, too.

I grew up with these ideals and goals. That was the easy part of working with wild things. The hard part—the almost ridiculous part—was finding a way to feed myself and my children while I did it. The possibilities are a little better today. At least now, when I speak to students with that familiar yearning in their eyes, I can tell them that, yes, it is possible to generate a salary as a rehabber. But certainly not in the normal sense of the term. If you want to get paid for what you do, instead of being a volunteer, you'll have to raise the money yourself. And once you do that, you're a professional.

Fifteen years ago I became the first professional wildlife rehabber in the state of Pennsylvania, and one of only a few in the entire country. Now, I'm happy to say, there are more of us. There also are some courses available in wildlife care. Basically, however, wildlife rehabbers are self-taught. We learn by observing, by reading, listening, and picking up information in any way we can. And we learn from that most severe teacher of all, our mistakes. But we're getting very good at what we do. We're getting so good at working with some species, such as falcons, that when they're endangered due to man's hastening of the evolutionary process, we can undo some of the hastening. We know what the birds need to get back into their natural habitat and survive in it.

Mostly, though, the job of a wildlife rehabber is to change the way people think about the natural world. Man isn't the boss of this planet. We only live here, along with many other forms of life. The more we understand about them, the more we'll know about ourselves and where we fit into the universe. A rehabber's greatest obstacle is an attitude of "Let nature take its course," "Don't get involved," "Somebody'll sue," "Don't give," "Don't share," "Don't love," "Don't care." We answer that not in words, but in the work we do. When we can save an orphaned fawn from starvation, or heal the bones of a muskrat hit by a car, or watch a hawk soar and glide and then land safely on legs that once were caught in a leg-hold trap, we're saying, *It's okay to care, it's okay to get involved, we can make a tiny difference.*

—Mary Jane Stretch
The Aark
Newtown, Pennsylvania

Acknowledgments

So many men, women, children, animals, and birds have been an important part of The Aark's existence and its future. I wish I could thank them individually, but I don't know them all by name. I hope they will realize what a warm place they have in my life and in this book.

My special gratitude goes to:

Papa Goose, who has been with me for fourteen years ever since his broken wings didn't heal well enough for him to fly. He was my first foster-parent, and to this day he makes it possible for me to double the number of orphaned baby ducks and geese I can care for because he literally takes them under his wing as soon as they are old enough to follow him around the barnyard.

To Mama Goose, recently deceased, who was brought in shortly after Papa Goose and with similar injuries; she was my second foster-parent and a dear friend.

To Donald Stretch, my husband, for being so patient and supportive when my work invaded our privacy and made demands on our time together.

To my daughters, Deborah Kovitch, Leah Soscia, and Samantha Martin, for their constant love and for being my bestest friends ever.

204

To Roy Frock, for teaching me how to handle hawks; learning to respect them was part of my education.

To Rosalie Neisley, my first volunteer, who convinced me that I couldn't do everything myself, and who left me wondering how I could do anything without her; the accident that took her life at such a young age created a loss that was shared by everyone who knew her.

To Dr. Thomas Fitzpatrick, for believing in my work and for being the first professional person to lend a hand.

To William Rossbauer, whose vision changed The Aark from a passion to a profession; he was the first business person on our roster of supporters.

To Dr. Paul Lanctot and Dr. Saul Neubauer, veterinarians, who are always on hand when I get in over my head, and who have given so freely of their time and patience.

To Maia Pennink Neely, for her devotion to The Aark, for all the time and interest she has put into our work, and for the boost she gave to our finances.

To Noreen Pallanta, for helping me through one of the most difficult years of my life.

To Paul B. Thomas, who runs our support league and makes my "Excedrin headaches" disappear.

To Diane Nickerson, for her cherished assistance in the present; and for the dedication and foresight that is taking The Aark into the future.

To all those who have worked beside me, past and present, in good times and bad, staying for a few months or a few years . . . cleaning cages, feeding baby birds and animals at all hours of the day and night, and sometimes just standing by silently when they knew I needed them to be there . . . how very important they are.

To everyone who stops to pick up a bird or an animal that needs help and brings it in to us; to the many kind souls who give, asking nothing, and who are such a vital part of The Aark; we have touched each other's lives and sometimes changed them.

Appendix
How to Be a
Friend to Wildlife

If you want to make your own environment a better habitat for wildlife, there are many simple things you can do, and your life will be the richer for it.

Inviting Wildlife In

If you live in an area where houses or apartments are close together, use birdfeeders. You'll attract more than birds. If your community is brand-new, you may not see many small animals at first, but as people settle in, the animal population that was displaced by development will begin to return. Raccoons, squirrels, skunks, opossums, and rabbits, as well as birds, co-exist in close proximity to human beings with no problem at all.

If you want to attract only certain birds and animals, then don't feed at all. The wild things will live without you. Obviously certain feeds attract certain species, but the issue is: either you like wildlife or you don't. They all have to eat. So if your mission is to feed—feed.

Plant shrubbery—thick, heavy types, like hedges—around the perimeters of your property to give wild animals a place where they can scoot and hide. Shrubs offer birds a haven, too, as well as a place to build their nests.

If you have enough space in your yard, you can set some of it apart and let it go wild. Or you can plant wildflowers, which actually are weeds. It may take two or three years for your wild area to get going, and during the first year it will look pretty unkempt, but later results will be gorgeous. And it's a perfect place for wildlife to live.

I'm in favor of a tidy yard, but you can have that, too, if you mark off your wild area with a simple fence. This makes it obvious that your boundaries are deliberate and that you are not a lazy groundskeeper.

Your feeders should hang free. Don't hang them close to bushes were cats and other predators can hide.

If starlings and grackles are chasing away smaller, more delicate birds, separate your feeding areas. Hang some thistle feeders and sunflower feeders in another area for the less aggressive birds.

Once you start feeding birds, it's important to keep it up. Sometimes it takes a while for the birds to discover the feeder, but when they do, they become dependent on it as a source of food. This is especially important in winter.

You need to keep your feeders clean, but you don't have to do it every day. After a rain or freeze, be sure to remove the feed that's stuck in the bottom so it doesn't ferment and get moldy. You don't have to wash the feeders. I use an old spatula to scrape out any food that's stuck in the bottom or corners. If you want to wash the feeder, use plain water and let it dry thoroughly in the sun before filling it. *Do not use bleaches or soaps.*

Water is even more important for wildlife than food. In winter, and in times of drought and extreme heat, there's always more food than water available. If you do nothing but put water out for birds and animals, you'll be doing a lot to help wildlife.

I put water in a regular birdbath, but I also put water on the ground, because some birds don't like to go high up. On the ground I use the clay basin of a bird bath without the pedestal. In summer, people often forget about water, or they think birdbaths are just pretty to look at and don't serve a practical purpose. But birds and animals need water. I can't tell you how many wild things come in to drink out of my ground-level basin. Even deer come in to drink. If you could set up a camera to record what comes in to drink your water at night, you would be astounded and delighted.

I always figure that if I don't want to drink the water in a birdbath, nobody else does, either. If you have a birdbath, keep it filled with clean water. Scrub it often with a stiff brush, but don't use detergent, soap, or bleach.

Keep your birdbath out in the open, but near a tree where the birds can perch safely. Don't place it near shrubs or other low plantings where predators might lurk. When birds get wet, they can't get away fast. They need to hop onto something quickly—but not something that covers them so much that they can't see what's coming. I keep my bird bath near an arborvitae, which has open space around the bottom of its trunk, but plenty of tiny branches where birds can perch.

It's especially important to keep water supplied in the cold of winter, yet this is just when people often stop putting it out because it freezes. The solution is to add glycerine—one tablespoon to a gallon of water. You can buy it in a feed store, and it doesn't cost much. In severe cold spells, some of the water may freeze, but there will always be a few small spots that stay open. In extreme circumstances you can also add hot water.

Now there are heaters available for birdbaths, and they

use very little electricity. It's a simple, inexpensive way to give wildlife what they need most, all year round.

Suet is for meat-eating birds—a replacement for the bugs some birds eat in summer. But use it only in winter; in warm weather it gets smelly and rancid, and birds won't eat it. Suet attracts some aggressive birds such as woodpeckers and starlings, so hang it out away from the area where smaller birds feed.

Salt bricks are good for many kinds of animals. Some are apple-flavored and very popular. If you don't want deer eating up your garden, put the salt brick in a field or an area away from your shrubs.

In the fall, as the holidays approach, if you want to include your wild friends in your festivities, you can do it in a way that's healthful and decorative at the same time. Popcorn, cranberries, apple chunks, and pieces of oranges and grapefruit can be strung and draped on a fence. Many animals love that kind of food. You can buy dried ears of corn at a feed mill and put them on sticks set in the ground. Squirrels and deer will eat the kernels right off the cob. Remember, though, to keep an eye on the fresh fruit and change it if it gets mushy before it gets eaten.

When winter is coming on, I cut open a fifty-pound bag of sweet pony feed and dump it near a big tree far enough away from my house where uninvited guests won't be a problem. The feed contains oats, molasses, and many other ingredients wild animals love, and it takes all winter for it to disappear. It's interesting to see how many different birds and animals come in to eat as the feed changes and ferments, as some of the seeds germinate and send up little green shoots.

If you have a small quiet area where you can dump a small amount of sweet feed and watch it from a distance, I can guarantee you'll have an interesting, educational winter.

Avoiding Bad Habits

If you're thinking in terms of the wildlife in your backyard, you should also think about where to put your trash and how to secure it from animal break-ins. If a lot of wild animals come in to raid your trash and make a mess of it, your property will become the neighborhood eyesore—and that isn't good public relations nor does it make a good advertisement for your support of wildlife.

Skunks and opossums can be kept out of trash if you use trashcans with locking lids and keep the cans closed. Raccoons, however, are not so easily discouraged. They're incredibly clever little animals that will work very hard to undo a lock, and an ordinary one won't stand up to their assaults. And with the current level of rabies in 'coons, you don't want to encourage them to visit.

The following precautions should help you keep your property neat:

• Don't leave trash around the edges of your property. It's an invitation to raiders.
• Put your trash in a sturdy can with a tight-fitting cover.
• Don't overload the can so the cover doesn't fit tightly.
• For an extra measure of security, fasten an elastic cord over the lid, down through the handles, and hook it securely on each side.

Unfortunately, your birdfeeders also invite raccoons, who come for the corn and sunflower seeds. Every night my feeders get torn apart by 'coons that have learned how to take the lids off. If they can't get them off, they rip the feeders apart. They'll hang on the feeder while they work at getting it open, and their weight adds to their effectiveness. People usually blame squirrels for the damage, but more often it's done by 'coons. Squirrels chew holes that get bigger and bigger, but they can't dismantle feeders the way 'coons do.

Be careful not to put out too much birdseed in warm weather, or you'll attract rats and mice—and they are not the kind of animals you'll want in your backyard. Neither will your neighbors. You'll also attract rodents if you scatter a lot of seed on the ground.

If you don't want to attract rats and mice:

• Place your birdfeeder where you can see it from a window, but away from your house, or you'll invite rodents to scoot under your foundation.
• Don't keep piles of wood near your house, your feeder, or your neighbor's house. They're a natural habitat for rats and mice.
• Keep your feeding areas clean by raking them once a week. Debris attracts rodents.
• Instead of sprinkling seeds on the ground for your ground feeders, put their seeds in a tray and set it on the ground. It'll be less messy that way. You can also make this simple screen feeder for them: Fasten a piece of window screening to four four-inch wooden dowels to lift the screen off the ground. Put your seeds on it. Water and snow will go through the screening, but the seeds won't. Ground-feeding birds won't have any trouble getting up on it. They'll spill some seed over the sides as they eat, but it won't be much and you can rake it up.

A screen feeder is also good for squirrels. And if you don't want them chewing up your feeders, put their peanuts and feed in another area.

Do not give peanut butter to birds and animals! Many people think that's a good thing to do—and the wild things love it—but I can't tell you how many times I find a glob of peanut butter stuck in the throat of a sick bird somebody brings in. Think about it. What happens when you swallow a spoonful of peanut butter? You spend the next ten minutes trying to get your tongue off the roof of your mouth. What makes you think a small animal doesn't have the same problem and then some? Peanut butter is oily; it gets on a bird's feathers; it's sticky; it confuses a bird's mouth, and gets in the way of its tongue. Plus, the bird can't understand what's happening to it. A small bird could be stressed to the point where it dies. If you want to give birds a treat, give them peanut hearts. They're nutritious, and the birds love them.

Discouraging Unwanted Visitors

If wildlife is a nuisance and you don't want to attract it, face up to it and don't make apologies. With a little effort, you can establish barriers that are sensible and safe for everyone.

Deer can be devastating to a garden. But people often move out into the deer's area to get away from the city, plant everything the deer love to eat, and then get mad because the deer eat it. You have to educate yourself about what deer like and refrain from planting it. Otherwise you're inviting deer in. If you don't want them eating your shrubs, find out what deer don't like, and plant accordingly. There are books on the subject, and any good nursery can give you the information you need. It's a matter of taking the time and caring enough to learn.

The deer in my area nibble away at the English ivy winding around the trunk of a big old tree outside my house. Now the tree looks like a giant mushroom, because as far up as the deer can reach, the ivy has been eaten away. But that doesn't bother me in the least. I get to watch the deer at night. I hear them bumping their backsides against the wall of my house while they eat. And it's wonderful! Sometimes I see as many as ten deer under my bedroom window.

The deer never bother with my hedges—but the bees do. When the hedges go into flower, I can't walk out my back door because the air is swarming with bees. So I'd rather have the deer. Of course, not everyone feels this way. So, if you live in an area that's heavy with deer, be clever in your planting.

There are sprays available to deter deer, but I've never heard of one that works. When I was a child, people used to say that dried human blood spread around the perimeter of a garden would keep rabbits and deer out, but as far as I know, it never worked, either. Nor did human hair. The old-fashioned scarecrow seems to work as well as anything. If something flaps in the wind—and if you move it occasionally—it will scare off wild things. But if you leave it in one place, the animals will get wise to it eventually.

Whether we want to get close to wildlife or keep a little distance between us, that's our choice. But the planet is meant for us to share. Getting to know our animal neighbors and understanding how their needs coincide with our own can be a delightful experience, one that teaches us not only about them, but about ourselves. Perhaps it can teach us how to save the earth.

Where to Go for Help

There is probably a wildlife rehabilitator in your area, but you may not find one listed in the telephone book. The reason is simple: most of us can't afford to advertise. But today many community agencies know where we are and they can direct you to us. If you come across a bird or a wild animal in need of help, contact your local police department, a veterinarian, a nature center, the SPCA, or a conservation officer and ask for the telephone number of your nearest rehabber.

A special note to the reader: While it's helpful and enjoyable to share our environment with wildlife, don't try to hold on to them or turn them into pets. In most states it is illegal to keep wildlife unless you have a permit to do so. This restriction is intended for the well-being of wild birds and animals. They need to be free. If you really care for them, their freedom should be your ultimate goal.